Waggoner on the Gospel of John

As Reprinted from The Present Truth
December 22, 1898 through June 1, 1899

By Ellet J. Waggoner

TEACH Services, Inc.
PUBLISHING
www.TEACHServices.com • (800) 367-1844

World rights reserved. This book or any portion thereof may not be copied or reproduced in any form or manner whatever, except as provided by law, without the written permission of the publisher, except by a reviewer who may quote brief passages in a review.

This book was written to provide truthful information in regard to the subject matter covered. The author assumes full responsibility for the accuracy of all facts and quotations as cited in this book. The opinions expressed in this book are the author's personal views and interpretation of the Bible, Spirit of Prophecy, and/or contemporary authors and do not necessarily reflect those of TEACH Services, Inc.

This book is sold with the understanding that the publisher is not engaged in giving spiritual, legal, medical, or other professional advice. If authoritative advice is needed, the reader should seek the counsel of a competent professional.

Copyright © 2013 TEACH Services, Inc.
ISBN-13: 978-1-4796-0053-3 (Paperback)
ISBN-13: 978-1-4796-0054-0 (ePub)
ISBN-13: 978-1-4796-0055-7 (Kindle/Mobi)

Library of Congress Control Number: 2012953397

Published originally in England as articles in the magazine, *The Present Truth*. Original British spelling retained.

Published by

www.TEACHServices.com • (800) 367-1844

Table of Contents

Preface	v
Christ the Beginning	7
"Follow Me"	13
Revealing The Glory	18
The New Birth	22
The Water Of Life	26
Healing The Nobleman's Son	31
Man's Rightful Authority	36
Christian Giving	42
Living By The Father	48
The Test Of Truth	53
How Not To Believe	58
The Good Shepherd	62
Saved And Kept	66
The Glory Of God	70
The Anointing At Bethany	74
Jesus Teaching Humility	77
Words Of Comfort	85
The Comforter	95
The Vine And The Branches	100
The Wondrous Name	104
Denying The Lord	109
The King Before The Judgment Bar	114
A Finished Work	118
Christ Risen	124

Preface

The apostle John, writing as the last of the New Testament authors, gave the world the most profound insight of any Bible writer into the mission of the Son of God to this world as our Saviour.

His Gospel more clearly and deeply probes the depth of pain Christ suffered from the rejection by "church leadership" of the people He came to save. Few if any theologians who write learned commentaries on the Gospel of John can write from personal fellowship with Christ in His sufferings.

The Lord gave Ellet J. Waggoner an unusual perspective on John's Gospel inasmuch as he had the task of enduring for years severe and unjust rejection from his contemporary brethren in ministry. The heart pain he was called to suffer forged for him a special link to the apostle's Gospel. In his unique individual way, Waggoner could at least begin to resonate. He was forced for years to meditate on the rejection and suffering Christ had to endure.

The result is a most unusual "commentary" on the Gospel of John, not a cademically exhaustive verse-by-verse, but more heart-warming as a series of inspirational meditations. They were written thoughtfully over a six-month period.

Best of all, Waggoner sought to be like his Lord in that he never became bitter or resentful. He followed Jesus' instructions to "pray for them which despitefully use you and persecute you." Thus a sunlit ray of Christlike love illuminates Waggoner's pages on John's Gospel.

Robert J. Wieland

Chapter 1
Christ the Beginning

"In the beginning was the Word, and the Word was with God, and the Word was God. The same was in the beginning with God. All things were made by Him; and without Him was not anything made that was made."

This Divine Word appeared in the person of Jesus of Nazareth; for "the Word was made flesh, and dwelt among us," and John bore witness of Him, saying, "He that cometh after Me is preferred before me; for He was before me."

This settles the question of the pre-existence of Christ, for all who have any respect for the Bible as the Word of God. It is true enough that the flesh of Jesus, that is, His fleshly body, was not in the beginning with God, the Creator of all things; for "when He cometh into the world, He saith, Sacrifice and offering Thou wouldst not, but a body hast Thou prepared for Me." Heb. 10:5. But "the flesh profiteth nothing;" it is the Spirit that quickeneth; and the life that animated the flesh of Jesus, and which is the real person, was the Word which was in the beginning with God, and which was God. So while cavillers may amuse themselves by playing upon words, we rejoice in the full assurance that this Jesus is the only begotten Son of God, the brightness of the Father's glory, and the express image of His person.

Jesus Christ Himself is the Beginning. Col. 1:18. He is "the beginning of the creation of God." Rev. 3:14. He is the power of God, and "the wisdom of God." 1 Cor. 1:24. Therefore it is He who speaks in the eighth chapter of Proverbs, saying, "I walk in the way of righteousness, in the midst of the paths of judgment; that I may cause those that love Me to inherit substance, and that I may fill their treasuries. The Lord possessed Me in the beginning of His way, before His works of old. I was set up from everlasting, from the beginning, or ever the earth was." Prov. 8:20-23.

On this last text it may be remarked that the words "set up" are from one Hebrew word meaning anointed, so that the meaning is the same as in the second Psalm, "Yet have I set My King upon My holy hill of Zion." The word is the same in the Hebrew, and it will be noticed in the margin we have "anointed" as the rendering of the Hebrew. Thus we learn that Christ was the anointed King before the earth existed.

Moreover, the word "in" has really no place in the twentieth verse of Proverbs 8, as there is nothing in the Hebrew to indicate it. So we read, "The Lord possessed Me, the Beginning of His way, before His works of old." Still further, it should be stated that the word "possessed" is the very same that occurs in Gen. 4:1, where we read that on the birth of Cain, Eve said, "I *have gotten* a man from the Lord." Therefore putting all these things together, we learn that Jesus was brought forth "from the days of eternity" (Micah 5:2, margin), before anything was created, and that He Himself is the beginning of all the ways of God. He is "the image of the invisible God, the firstborn of all creation." Col. 1:15. He is the Beginning of everything.

The Firstborn

"Whom He did foreknow, He also did predestinate to be conformed to the image of His Son, that He might be the firstborn among many brethren." Rom. 8:29. "As many as received Him, to them gave He power to become the sons of God, even to them that believe on His name." John 1:12. This is why we rejoice in the fact that Jesus of Nazareth, who was "born of a woman, born under the law" (Gal. 4:4), is the Son of God. It shows us that although we are born to low estate, subject by nature to all the infirmities that are the inheritance of man born of woman, we may become sons of God, own brothers of the Lord Jesus Christ, and sharers of all His fullness.

Christ is the firstborn among many brethren. Thus He is the heir; but we are joint-heirs with Him. It is not as in earthly estates, where the eldest is the sole heir to the titles and estates, and the younger brothers must look out for themselves. Christ is indeed the heir to the titles and to all the estate of God; but there is no exclusiveness in Him. Whatever He has, He shares in equal measure with all His brethren. "Of His fullness have all we received." If we receive Him in His fullness, He gives us not only the privilege, but the power, the right, to be the sons of God. All that He is, we may be, but only in Him as the Beginning, the Author and Finisher of our faith, and therefore of our works. By the will of God, through the Blessed Spirit, we have the same rights that Christ Himself has.

"How can this be?" If you are wise, and would be wiser, you will not ask that question. Be content not to know so much as God, for you never can, no matter how much you try. Who can explain the mystery of life? "As thou knowest not what is the way of the Spirit, nor how the bones do grow in the womb of her that is with child; even so thou knowest not the works of God who maketh all." Eccl. 11:5. Yet nobody refuses to be called the son of his father, nor to inherit an estate that may fall to him as son, because he cannot understand the mystery of birth. Why should we be any more foolish in dealing with that new birth which makes us veritable sons of God? The "plan of salvation" is entirely beyond the comprehension of the human mind; but the working out, the results, of the plan, we may know by experience, provided we believe.

Jesus Christ is the firstborn among many brethren," the firstborn of all creation," because "in Him were all things created, in the heavens and upon the earth;" and it is for this reason that in Him we have redemption, even the forgiveness of our sins. Redemption is creation, for "if any man be in Christ, there is a new creation." We become sons of God, therefore, by the same power by which Christ, the Divine Word, created all things in the beginning. Now creation is not a fancy, but a fact. It is not a mere mental process, a conception, but a tangible reality, a thing done. It is done, however, solely by the Word of God. "For He spake, and it was, He commanded, and it stood fast." So the fact that we are as really sons of God as Christ is, rests on the same foundation as does the creation. It is all of Christ, "who is the beginning, the firstborn from the dead; that in all things He might have the pre-eminence."

The Will of God

"As many as received Him, to them gave He power to become the sons of God, even to them that believe on His name; which were born, not of blood, nor of the will of the flesh, nor of the will of man, but of God." John 1:12, 13. "Of His own will He brought us forth by the word of truth, that we should be a kind of firstfruits of His creatures." James 1:18.

Men commonly speak of the will of God as if it were something to be dreaded, and to be endured when it cannot be avoided. When they enjoy prosperity, or what seems to them to be prosperity, they take it as a matter of course; but when there is adversity they complain for a while, and then piously talk about submitting to the will of God. It is with them as though the will of God were exercised only to thwart us, and to make our lives a burden. On the contrary, the will of God is exercised to give us life and happiness. "It is not the will of your Father which is in heaven, that one of these little ones should perish."

"This is the will of God, even your sanctification." 1 Thess. 4:3. He says, "Be ye holy, for I am holy." 1 Peter 1:16. Certainly; that is most fitting; for the son is heir of the father. We are children of God, and if children, then heirs. So of course we must be holy, since holiness is His nature. To be sons of God means nothing else than to be partakers of the Divine nature. So as it is His will that we should be His sons, it is His will that we should be holy. His will is made known to us in His Word. When we hear His Word, we have simply to say from the heart, "Thy will be done," and it will be so, even as "it was so" when He spoke in creation, saying, Let this and that be. There is eternal power in the thought of God. Everything that we can see in the visible creation is but the product of His thought. So if we accept His thought, His will, we shall be made to the praise of the glory of His grace.

We had nothing to do with bringing ourselves into this world. We were born of flesh and blood, and of the will of man, but not of our own will. Now when we receive the Lord, not as a figure of speech, but as a real Person, really present with us through the eternal Spirit, by whom He offered Himself to God, His will makes us sons of God, deriving our whole life directly from the Lord as really as when we were born of the flesh we derived our lives from our parents.

"Ah, yes," some one says, "but that is spiritual; it is only spiritually that we are the sons of God." That is the language by which Satan makes people deny the truth even while pronouncing the words of truth. It is true that it is only spiritually that we are the sons of God, but that does not mean that we are not really and wholly the sons of God by faith in Christ Jesus. "They that are in the flesh cannot please God. But ye are not in the flesh, but in the Spirit, if so be that the Spirit of God dwell in you. Now if any man have not the Spirit of Christ, he is none of His. And if Christ be in you, the body is dead because of sin; but the Spirit is life because of righteousness." Rom. 8:8-10. Spiritual things are real, and may be handled. Christ was wholly spiritual, even when He walked this earth as a man, and in Him all who believe are made spiritual even while yet on this earth.

In Christ we are "builded together for an habitation of God through the Spirit." Eph. 2:22. Now of the living creatures forming the throne of God in the heavens, it is said, "They went, every one, straight forward; whither the Spirit was to go, they went." Eze. 1:12. God's thought is the law of their lives; it moves them. His Spirit of life is in them so that they have no existence, no thought apart from Him; as He think, so they are. Our prayer is to be, "Thy kingdom come; Thy will be done in earth, as it is in heaven." This is a possibility, else the Saviour would not have told us to pray for it. Let it be according to His word.

The Light of Life

"In Him was life; and the life was the light of men." "That was the true Light, which lighteth every man that cometh into the world." John 1:4, 9. Verses 3 and 4 are by some of the best scholars rendered thus: "All things were made by Him; and without Him was not anything made. That which was made in Him was life; and the life was the light of men." It is simply a difference in placing the marks of punctuation, which as is well known are no part of the original text. It is a fact that everything that is made in Him is life. Whoever is in Him must live, for He is life itself.

"And the light shineth in darkness; and the darkness comprehended it not." The margin of the Revised Version gives "overcame" in the place of "comprehended." Perhaps we can get a better grasp of the idea conveyed by this word "comprehend," by noting Isa. 40:12, where we are told that God "comprehended the dust of the earth in a measure." When we put a thing in a measure, it is shut in. Even so light may sometimes be shut in by darkness. Go out some foggy night in London; if you are not careful you may run against a lamp-post. Why? Because the thick fog so shuts in the rays that come from the lamp, that they do not reach more than a few inches. They are shut in as by a thick wall or put within a bushel. They cannot penetrate the gloom. The darkness comprehends or overcomes the light. But not so with the light of life. It shines out in the darkness, and the darkness does not prevail against it. That is a true light; it is of worth. It is not only unquenchable, but it cannot be kept within bounds of darkness.

A portion of this unquenchable life is in every man that comes into the world. It would all be in every man, if no man would reject it; for "of His fullness have all we received." But men "hold down the truth in unrighteousness." Rom. 1:18, R.V. Christ is the truth and the life. They work against the life, because they love death. Prov. 8:36. What wondrous grace has been manifested by the Lord, in that He has so marvelously provided for the salvation of all men. Upon every soul of mankind has He bestowed this wondrous love, that all might be called the sons of God. Men may reject the love, but that does not at all nullify the fact that it has been bestowed.

This light of life is in every man that comes into the world. It "lighteth every man coming into the world." R.V. As he comes into the world, he receives the light. It is ours from our earliest infancy. With our first breath we have the life of Christ. What for?—"The Word is very nigh unto thee, in thy mouth, and in thy heart, that thou mayest do it." Deut. 30:14. And this Word was in the beginning with God, and the Word was God. So although "the wicked are estranged from the womb; they go astray as soon as they be born, speaking lies" (Ps. 58:3), there is no excuse for their so doing. God's eternal power and Divinity are to be seen in them as well as in the other things that He has made, "that they may be without excuse." Rom. 1:19, 20. The life is with them from the very beginning, in order that they may live even as Christ lived.

Do you say that this but increases the condemnation of all mankind, in that all have sinned, and "there is none that doeth good, no, not one?" Very true, but "where sin abounded, grace did much more abound." Great as the condemnation may be, greater still is the salvation. The life is in every man, not for condemnation, but for salvation. "For God sent not His Son into the world to condemn the world; but that the world through Him might be saved." John 3:17. These things are for our learning, not for our discussion. They are not theories, but facts. We are to understand them by believing them, and thus we get life through His name.

—December 22, 1898

Chapter 2
"Follow Me"

"Again the next day after John stood, and two of his disciples; and looking upon Jesus as He walked, he saith, Behold the Lamb of God! And the two disciples heard him speak, and they followed Him." John 1:35-37.

"The day following Jesus would go forth into Galilee, and findeth Philip, and saith unto him, Follow Me." Verse 43.

That the disciples first mentioned did not follow the Lord without being called, is seen from the account in Matthew's Gospel. There we read: "And Jesus, walking by the Sea of Galilee saw two brethren, Simon called Peter, and Andrew his brother, casting a net into the sea; for they were fishers. And He saith unto them, Follow Me, and I will make you fishers of men. And they straightway left their nets, and followed Him." Matt. 4:18-20.

The first thing to be considered is that this call of Jesus is to us as well as to those of whom we read in this narrative. To all who labour, and are heavy laden, the Saviour says, "Come unto Me." "And the Spirit and the Bride say, Come. And Let him that heareth say, Come. And let him that is athirst come. And whosoever will, let him take the water of life freely." Rev. 22:17.

We are apt to lose the most of the blessing that we should receive from the narrative of the calling of the first disciples of Jesus, because we allow the story of what they became to drive from our minds the knowledge of what they were when they were called. We imagine that Jesus called them because of some special goodness in them, which drew Him to them, and so think that they were specially favoured above other men. Thus it is taken for granted that such ordinary mortals as we are could never be called by the Lord as they were called. Let us therefore see if we can find out anything about the nature of these men who were so honoured by the Lord as to be called to follow Him.

There were twelve of them, but of only a few have we any particulars. We know that Peter and Andrew and James and John were fishers. Fishing is not the most refined and gentle occupation in the world, and we are given glimpses of the character of James and John, which show that they were not very gentle by nature. They, as well as Peter, were ready to fight anyone who offered them or their Master insult.

When Peter was brought into the place where his life seemed to be endangered through his acquaintances with Christ, his fears gained the mastery of him, and he denied his Lord. Not only so, but he did it with curses and swearing. Now we cannot suppose that Peter was in the habit at that time of using profane language; but we well know that men who have never in their lives been accustomed to use such language, do not break forth into profane expletives on any occasion, no matter how much they are taken unawares. But a man who in former days has been in the habit of swearing, but who through association with Christ has abstained from it for some time, may very easily relapse into the old way when sudden temptation assaults him while away from the Lord. Indeed, no matter how long a man has been master of an evil habit, the moment he loses his connection with the Lord, that moment he begins to sink back into the old slough. So the fact that when Peter was frightened into denying Christ, he did it with cursing and swearing, shows that in the old days before he knew the Lord, he had been a rough, profane fisherman; full of generous impulses, and what the world would call "good hearted," but the very opposite of the Christian gentleman that he became when filled with the Spirit of God.

Judas as another of the men whom Jesus called. He was the one who betrayed the Lord, selling Him for thirty pieces of silver. His besetting sin was covetousness. When the funds of the little company of disciples were placed in his keeping, he became a thief. Yet we must not forget that he was called by the Lord to be an apostle, and as one of the twelve was sent out with "power over unclean spirits, to cast them out, and to heal all manner of disease and all manner of sickness," and was given the commission, "Heal the sick, raise the dead, cleanse the lepers, cast out devils." Matt. 10:1-8. Even up to the very moment when he delivered the Lord into the hands of the mob, there was no one but the Lord Himself who could distinguish any particular difference between him and the other disciples. He was outwardly as correct in his deportment as they; and there is nothing to indicate that in the beginning his nature was any worse than theirs. Indeed, from what the Bible teaches of the nature of all men, we know that when the disciples were called, Judas was as promising a subject as any of them.

What made the difference at the last?—Simply this, that the eleven yielded themselves to the influence of the Lord, and were drawn out of their old lives, and transformed by His Spirit, while Judas, however much he may have been attracted at the first, clung to his own way, stubbornly resisting the transforming power of the Lord, and so became more and more hardened. Judas shows what any man may come to if he resists the Spirit, while Peter, James, and John, together with many others, reveal to us what the grace of God can do for anyone who submits to it.

It is no disparagement of the apostles to say that by nature they were no better than any other men. They all, including Judas, had faculties which, when trained and developed by the Lord, would make them most powerful workers in His service, but which, left untrained, would make them equally strong to do evil. It is to the everlasting praise of the glory of the grace of the Lord Jesus, that such men, taken from such surroundings as they were taken, could develop into such giants in spiritual stature, and such able ministers of the Holy Spirit.

The lesson to be learned from the call of these disciples is one of hope, and courage, and trust. We are to remember that they were men "of like passions" with us, neither better nor worse by nature than we are. They may have had some more marked characteristics than we have, which would make them capable of occupying a larger sphere than we are designed for, but in that respect they did not differ from us more than many of our unbelieving fellow-men do at the present time; for there is no doubt that there are very many men in the world, who have greater *natural* ability than the majority of those who have given themselves to the Lord's service. We are to learn that what a man is by *nature* is not by any means the measure of what he may be by *grace*. Just to the extent that we, in our thought of what the most of the twelve became, lose sight of what they were when they were called, do we lose the benefit of the sacred narrative. It was written for *our* learning, that we through patience and comfort of the Scriptures might have hope. Since they were but sample specimens of all mankind, and God is no respecter of persons, we see in their call the call of all men. It rests with us, by humble acceptance of the will of God, to make our calling and election sure.

Object of the Call

Jesus said to the first disciples just what He says to all, "Follow Me." Now let us see why they were called. We have seen that when called they were sinners. Jesus did not call them for what they were, but for what they might become under His training. Did He therefore say, "Follow Me, and I will save you from your sins?"—That was implied in the call, but that is not what He said. What He said was, "Follow Me, and I will make you fishers of men." And that is just what His call means to every one of us. Personal salvation is included in the call, as a matter of course; for no one can give to others that which he has not himself; but that fact that Jesus calls us to Him in order that we may be saved is emphasized and made more sure by the fact that He calls us to make us saviours of others.

There are so many among professed followers of the Lord Jesus who are even after years of Christian profession often troubled with doubts as to their acceptance with God. They wish they knew that they were accepted of Christ. What wonder, then, that we find so many seekers after God who are appalled at the sense of their own unworthiness, and who hesitate to make a start to serve the Lord, fearing that He will not accept such sinners as they are. Now all these fears would be swept away if these persons could but be brought to see the fullness of the meaning of the call of the Lord Jesus. It does not stop with the individual who is called. God calls us, in order that through us He may reach somebody else. "Let him that heareth say, Come." So when anybody says, "It doesn't seem as though the Lord could save so great a sinner as I am," you may always say in reply, "My dear brother, or sister, the Lord has called you for the sole purpose of making you a saviour of some other poor sinner; the saving of you is incidental to that object. It is but a light thing for Him to save you; the great thing is that He will make you a means of salvation."

Let us now read one or two texts which make this even more clear. The first is 2 Cor. 5:17-20. We quote the margin of the Revision, and omit the word "you" from verse 20, which, as indicated by being placed in italics, is no part of the text. "If any man [person] is in Christ, there is a new creation; the old things are passed away; behold, they are become new. But all things are of God, who reconciled us to Himself through Christ, and gave unto us the ministry of reconciliation: to wit, that God was in Christ reconciling the world unto Himself, not reckoning unto them their trespasses, and having placed in us the word of reconciliation. We are ambassadors therefore on behalf of Christ, as though God were intreating by us; we beseech on behalf of Christ, be ye reconciled to God."

In reading this do not forget that the ones who have the word of reconciliation placed in them are the ones who are reconciled. Whoever therefore is in Christ, and therefore a new creature, has in him the word of reconciliation, and so is an ambassador for Christ, to carry on the ministry of reconciliation. By each one who accepts the Lord Jesus, God beseeches sinners even as He did by Him. If you have never seen this in the text, read it until you can see it, for it is there.

Now we will read Isa. 49:6-9: "It is a light thing that thou shouldest be My servant to raise up the tribes of Jacob, and to restore the preserved of Israel; I will also give thee for a light to the Gentiles, that thou mayest be My salvation unto the ends of the earth. Thus saith the Lord, the Redeemer of Israel, and His Holy One, to him whom man despiseth, to him whom the nation abhorreth, to a servant of rulers, Kings shall see and arise, princes also shall worship, because of the Lord that is faithful, and the Holy One of Israel, and He shall choose thee. Thus saith the Lord, In an acceptable time have I heard thee, and in a day of salvation have I helped thee; and I will preserve thee, and give thee for a covenant of the people, to establish the earth, to cause to inherit desolate heritages; that thou mayest say to the prisoners, Go forth; to them that are in darkness, Show yourselves."

There can be no question but that these words apply primarily to Christ; but He is "the Son of man," and came to earth in man's stead in order that we might be ambassadors in His stead. That these words refer to men whom the Lord calls, equally with Christ, may be seen by comparing verse 6 with Acts 13:46, 47, where we read that Paul and Barnabas said, "We turn to the Gentiles. For so hath the Lord commanded us, saying, I have set thee to be a light of the Gentiles, that thou shouldst be for salvation unto the ends of the earth." The apostles applied the words to themselves as naturally as though they themselves had been named in the prophecy. This shows that whatever work was given to the Lord to do in this earth, is given to every one who will accept His call.

How wonderfully comforting is this scripture! To whom does the Lord say that He will make him His salvation? "To him whom man despiseth." It is true that Jesus was despised and rejected of men; but He was despised solely on our account, because He bore our reproach. He put Himself absolutely in the sinner's place. Yet despised as He was, as one forsaken of the Lord for his sins, He was the salvation of God, showing that every one who is despised for sins that he himself has done is also chosen to be the salvation of God.

What a blessed sound is the call of the Lord! How it removes every shade of doubt and fear. No longer, when we rightly hear it, is there any room for doubt if the Lord can save us. The call of the Lord reaches far beyond that, saying to us as it finds us in the degradation of sin, "Son, go work today in My vineyard." "Be ye therefore followers of God as dear children."

—December 29, 1898

Chapter 3
Revealing The Glory

There were three different occasions when Jesus on earth is said to have manifested His glory. The first was at a wedding feast in Cana of Galilee; the second was when He took Peter, James and John into an high mountain apart, and was transfigured before them; and the third was at the grave of Lazarus. These are to show us that it is not merely when we go apart from the world, that the glory of God may appear to us, and be manifested in us, but when we are engaged in the most common affairs of life. Since the earth is full of His glory, it is most fitting that it should at all times be revealed. Even so it is to all and in all who believe.

Jesus was about thirty years of age when He began His public ministry. Before that time we have only one glimpse of Him, for a single day when He was twelve years old, and as a son of the synagogue was allowed to engage in the temple worship. Then follow eighteen years of work at the carpenter's bench, entirely lost to public view. A mighty work was committed to Him, and from earliest childhood He knew that He must be about His Father's business, yet He seems to have made no haste to appear in public. Shall we say that He was not doing His Father's business all the time? Not by any means. What a lesson to us, who are so prone to think that we are not doing any active service for the Master unless we are engaged in some public service. And then note how often in the very short time He had for public labour, we find Him attending some feast or other. He never seems to have been in a hurry. Why not? The reason is that He dwelt in eternity, and laboured in its strength. He who has all eternity, need never be flurried; even so with Him who labours with the power of an endless life. But whether attending a wedding feast or preaching to the multitudes, Jesus was about His Father's business. The glory of God was always revealed, whether He ate or drank or preached.

The wine gave out, but what mattered that when the true wine was present? The element of time does not count in any of the Lord's works. One day is with the Lord as a thousand years. Then how easy for Him to accelerate the process of the production of wine by the grapevine, and do the work of a year in a minute. The thing which Jesus did—turning water into wine—is what He does every year. The rain falls from heaven, the earth receives it, and the rootlets of the vine drink it up. Then by the warmth and sunlight it is drawn up and deposited in the clusters and transformed into delicious wine. Do not forget that "the new wine is found in the cluster." Isa. 65:8. It is wine while it is yet sealed up in the skin of the grape. Just as the fruit, if it is bruised and broken and exposed to the air, soon decays, and becomes unfit for food, so does the wine, when taken from its original flask, in which it is hermetically sealed, and exposed to the air so that it ferments, become unfit for human consumption.

Suppose any man should be asked to take a glass of water, and turn it into wine; the request would be in vain. Well, do not ask him to do it instantly; give him a year in which to perform the task. That is no better; at the close of the year he would be no nearer the completion of his task than at the beginning. Let him have ten years, a hundred years; the result is the same—nothing. Moreover, he cannot tell how it is done. Thus we see that the miracle does not consist in the fact that the water was turned into wine instantly, but in the fact that it was done at all. The miracle that is performed every year by what is called "natural growth" is as great as the miracle at Cana of Galilee. That was done in a way to call attention to the fact that it is Jesus who produces the fruits of the earth. In taking the pure "blood of the grape," as well as of any other fruit, we are taking the life of Christ. The blood is the life, and when Jesus took the cup at the last supper, He said, "This is My blood."

It is not an infrequent thing to hear or read of some reformed drunkard who has had the old taste revived by the wine used at the communion service, and has relapsed into the old habits; and others dare not partake for fear of the consequences. Shall we say that it was the blood of Christ that caused him to fall? Impossible! His blood does not lead into sin, but cleanses from all sin. No; that was not "the Lord's Supper." Nobody ever gets drunk or tempted to drunkenness at the Lord's table. The fermented wine that is by some thought to be absolutely essential to the observance of the Lord's Supper, has nothing whatever in common with "the precious blood of Christ, as of a Lamb without blemish and without spot," by which we are redeemed. The cup that could by any possibility make the tenderest child or the most delicate woman intoxicated, or that can arouse slumbering passions in any man, is not the communion of the blood of Christ, but "the cup of devils." It is not the cup of blessing, but the cup of cursing. It is a terrible thing thus to misrepresent Christ. He provides only that which gives life and peace.

"This beginning of miracles did Jesus in Cana of Galilee, and manifested forth His glory; and His disciples believed on Him." There was no transfiguration scene here. The person of Jesus did not shine; there was nothing about Him that anybody could see any more than with the other guests at the feast. Yet He manifested forth His glory. So we see that power—the power of God, which works miracles—is glory. Power and glory are synonymous in God's vocabulary. In Eph. 1:17–20 we read of the working of God mighty power, by which he raised Jesus from the dead. In Rom. 6:4 we are told that "Christ was raised up from the dead by the glory of the Father." Thus we see that God's power is His glory. We are to be "strengthened with all power according to the might of His glory." Col. 1:11. "According to the riches of His glory" we are to be "strengthened with might by His Spirit." Eph. 3:16.

"There is no power but of God." There is but one force in the universe, and that is the life of the Lord; but there are an infinite variety of manifestations of it. We ourselves are daily witnesses of the fact that glory—visible glory, light—is power. The huge steamship with its hundreds of passengers, and thousands of tons of freight, is driven across the ocean by engines that are fed with coal that in a few days gives off the accumulated sunlight of centuries. The forest trees had for centuries absorbed the sunlight, and now they give it forth in one great blaze which is seen to be power. God's people are "trees of righteousness," growing by the light of "the Sun of Righteousness." "It doth not yet appear what we shall be" any more than the trunk of the oak shows the careless passer-by the glory that is stored up within; but when the Lord comes the glory will be revealed, for "then shall the righteous shine forth as the sun in the kingdom of their Father." Matt. 13:43. But in the meantime their glory is manifested forth in good works which God does by them. "Let your light so shine before men, that they may see your good works, and glorify your Father which is in heaven."

The mother of Jesus said to the servants: "Whatsoever He saith unto you, do it." We do not know their names, yet they had an active part in the performance of the miracle. They brought the water and filled the vessels, and they drew out the wine. If we are His servants, ready to do His bidding, He will use us in the performance of many mighty works. When the thousands of hungry people were in the desert, Jesus said to His disciples, "Give ye them to eat," and so they did. All the vast multitudes received food at the hands of the twelve; but they received it from the Lord of life and glory. To us comes the command, "Hear Him!" Whatsoever He saith unto you do it, without asking any questions. If the servants of that house in Cana had refused to fill the water pots with water, because they could not see how any good could come from it, the miracle would have been performed, but they would have been disgraced. Let us beware of losing our opportunity through doubt and hesitation, and the glory of His wondrous deeds will at the last be shared with us.

—January 5, 1899

Chapter 4
The New Birth

John 3:1–16

There was a man of the Pharisees, named Nicodemus, a ruler of the Jews; the same came to Jesus by night, and said unto Him, Rabbi, we know that Thou art a teacher come from God; for no man can do these miracles that Thou doest, except God be with him." John 3:1, 2.

It is well when those who have the truth of God have such power with them that men cannot fail to see that God is with them. God has promised that it shall be so, and that means that He expects it to be so. He says to His people, concerning the men of earth: "They shall fall down unto thee, and make supplication unto thee, saying, Surely, God is in thee; and there is none else, there is no God." Isa. 45:14. When the Jewish Sanhedrin talked with Peter and John, they gave the credit of their boldness to the Lord. Acts 4:13. So when a great miracle was wrought by the agency of Peter, "all that lived at Lydda and Saron saw him and turned to the Lord." Acts 9:35, 42. The true servant of Jehovah, no matter how great the work he does, always leads the people to think of his Master. "Let your light so shine before men, that they may see your good works, and glorify your Father, which is in heaven." Matt. 5:16.

In the address of Nicodemus, however, we can see an intended compliment to the Man Jesus, such as most people feel it their duty to give to the minister. "I liked that sermon; it expressed just what I have always believed." "There is no doubt but that you are doing a grand work here; your preaching is having a great influence on the people." Now while it is always right to encourage a man, the best way in the world to encourage a servant of Christ is to give personal heed to what he says, and let the fruits be seen in the life. Too many think that their duty is fully discharged if they assent to what is said, having no thought that it means that they must make any change in their lives. How often this Scripture is fulfilled: "And as for thee, son of man, the children of thy people talk of thee by the walls and in the doors of the houses, and speak one to another, every one to his brother, saying, Come, I pray you, and hear what is the word that cometh forth from the Lord. And they come unto thee as the people cometh, and they sit before thee as My people, and they hear thy words, but they do them not: for with their mouth they show much love, but their heart goeth after their gain. And, lo, thou art unto them as a very lovely song of one that hath a pleasant voice, and can play well on an instrument: for they hear thy words, but they do them not." Eze. 33:30–32. They praise the singer and the song, but they do not have any thought that it is more than a thing merely to listen to.

Jesus cut short the compliment of Nicodemus. All that Nicodemus said was true, and we may believe that he was sincere in saying it; but Jesus did not care to talk about Himself or His work. Very abrupt and ungracious His words doubtless seemed to Nicodemus, in response to his polite greeting. The ruler had praised Jesus, and had not the slightest idea but that Jesus would feel gratified on account of his attention, for he had no thought that he was anything but a model; but Jesus instantly responded: "Except a man be born again he cannot see the kingdom of God."

What! a Pharisee, a ruler of the Jews, one who from his youth up had been trained in the law, and who always exercised himself to preserve a conscience void of offence toward men and toward God; must such an one be wholly made new before he can be saved? "Verily, verily, I say unto thee, except a man be born again, he cannot see the kingdom of God." Nicodemus knew that the Lord meant him, and he knew that the sentence meant a complete transformation of life, and the implied rebuke nettled him, so that he affected not to understand it, and began to quibble. Notice that Jesus did not pay any attention to his question, "How can a man be born when he is old?" except to repeat the statement. He did not attempt any explanation in answer to the question, "How can these things be?" but simply assured him of the fact. No one can explain the mystery of the natural birth; why then should anyone stumble over the mystery of the new birth?

The statement is sweeping: Nobody can enter the kingdom of heaven except by a new birth. The birth that brings us into the kingdom of men, does not introduce us into the kingdom of God. Nobody is born a Christian. No matter how godly a person's ancestry may have been, nor into how pious a home he may be born, he must be born again, or he cannot be saved. Pious parents are a blessing, and a wonderful help in the way of life; but there is a work that must be accomplished in every individual soul by the Holy Spirit alone. The child who has truly God-fearing parents must grow up to be a Christian, and should become one very young; but nobody is born a Christian. He may have learned Scripture language as a matter of course, from hearing so much, and may never have heard words of scoffing or profanity. He may have been trained from earliest infancy to read the Bible and to engage in family and public religious exercises. All this is good, but nothing that anybody can get from human beings from first to last, no matter how closely related or how good, can take the place of the personal work of the Holy Spirit in the heart. As great a blessing as pious training is, if it is depended on as being sufficient, the individual is in a worse condition than the one who has never known religious associations, and who knows that he is a worthless sinner.

"That which is born of the flesh is flesh, and that which is born of the Spirit is Spirit." "Marvel not that I said unto thee, Ye must be born again," or "from above." "The wind bloweth where it listeth, and thou hearest the sound thereof, but canst not tell whence it cometh nor whither it goeth; so is every one that is born of the Spirit." The wind bloweth where it will, and yet it has no will of itself; it comes from God and returns to God, according to His will; so in every one that is born of the Spirit. He maketh His angels winds. In these words of Christ we have not merely the mystery of the process of new birth set forth, but we have a suggestion of the wondrous power to be manifested in those born of the Spirit. Don't try to explain, and don't reason from your own past experience, nor even from anything that you have seen. Do you not know that by trying to understand how these things can be, before we accept them, we limit the amount of blessing that we are to receive, to our own comprehension; whereas God wishes to do for us "exceeding abundantly above all that we ask or think?" "Eye hath not seen, nor ear heard, neither have entered into the heart of man, the things which God hath prepared for them that love Him. But God hath revealed them unto us by His Spirit; for the Spirit searcheth all things, yea, the deep things of God." 1 Cor. 2:9, 10. Yield to God's will, and you will know things that no human language can tell you.

Nothing is plainer in the Scriptures than that all the disabilities which we inherit by birth from our parents are counteracted and overcome by the birth from the Spirit. We inherit sinful dispositions. It is not the specific acts of sin that a man has committed, that will cause his everlasting destruction, so much as it is the evil nature that is in him, even if it has not manifested itself in any way that is noticeable by men. We have the evil in us, and always with us, and again and again we have said, "It's no use; I cannot possibly overcome this sin; it is a part of my very being," and have felt almost in despair, or else we have apologized for the hateful thing by saying, "Oh, it's only my way; I don't mean anything bad by it; but I simply can't help it; and God will not hold me responsible for what I am not to blame for. I had this way from birth." Now read: "As by the offence of one, judgment came upon all men to condemnation; even so by the righteousness of One the free gift came upon all men unto justification of life. For as by one man's disobedience many were made sinners, so by the obedience of One shall many be made righteous." Rom. 5:18, 19.

The New Birth

We are not responsible for having been born sinners. Since all our ancestors were sinners, it was inevitable that we should be born sinners if born at all; and we had no voice in the matter of our birth; therefore God does not hold us responsible. But that does not mean that He excuses the sin, and holds our being sinners as a light thing. No; He does not hold us responsible for the sin; for "God was in Christ, reconciling the world unto Himself, not imputing their trespasses unto them." 2 Cor. 5:19. And this reconciliation is effected by undoing all the evil that was entailed on us by our first birth. Because God does not hold us responsible for the sin that is born in us, He provides for a new birth, direct from Himself, which will make us strong where we were weak by nature. We are "heirs of God," of His Person and character, of all that He is and has. We cannot understand it, but the knowledge and belief of the fact makes us "strengthened with all might according to His glorious power."

Jesus spoke of Himself as "the Son of Man, which is in heaven," yet He was at that very moment talking to Nicodemus. He was always "in the bosom of the Father," so that we may know that He is with us now that He has ascended to heaven; and more, that we may see the possibility of dwelling in the secret place of God. He who abides in God can speak of heavenly things as of that which he knows and understands. There is no uncertainty in his testimony.

Everybody who is saved must believe many things that he cannot explain to anybody, not even to himself. How often the Bible teacher is met with the challenge or request to "harmonize" two statements in the Bible. "How can these things be?" is asked again and again. Now if he sets about trying to explain every *seeming* contradiction, and should refuse to accept a truth or take a step forward until he can reconcile it with everything else, he will land in total darkness. "By faith we understand." "He that believeth hath the witness in himself." Faith is not contrary to reason, but the things with which it deals are so infinitely above and beyond the range of human thought that one must have the mind of God in order to comprehend them. So it is useless to spend time arguing with an unbeliever or a questioner. Such time is wasted. Tell him the truth with all authority, and with such positiveness as can come only from close, personal knowledge, and which must carry conviction. If the man once believes, he will know for himself why you could not explain everything to him. If he will not believe, it makes no difference what he thinks of you or your ability.

—*January 12, 1899*

Chapter 5
The Water of Life

John 4:5–15

In the account of Christ's interview with the woman of Samaria, we have a striking example of His faithfulness to the mission entrusted to Him. He was hungry and weary with His journey, and as He rested by Jacob's well at noonday, His disciples having gone into Sychar to buy food, the woman came to draw water. His request that she would give Him some to drink was met by an expression of surprise on the part of the woman that He, being a Jew, should ask any favour from a Samaritan. Not a very encouraging opening, but beneath the exterior of superstition and ignorance, Christ recognized the spiritual need and longed to open to this benighted soul the treasure of the Father's love.

He did not ask her to come again when He would be feeling rested and refreshed, or suggested that, if she could get together a sufficient congregation to make it worth while, He would speak to them on some very important truths, but to this single individual He proceeded to make known His work and character. She did not seem a very hopeful subject, living in sin, her mind set on temporal advantages, only seeking the water of life if it would save her the trouble of coming to the well to draw water, and so far as one could judge from her trivial, irrelevant interruptions, entirely unresponsive to the deep spiritual truths which Jesus was unfolding to her. Yet this woman was among the very few to whom Christ explicitly stated that He was the Messiah. His words at last reached her heart. Spiritual things prevailed; she recognized in Christ the One whom she needed, and now, leaving her waterpot, she sought to bring her neighbors and friends into contact with the Saviour.

The woman of Samaria is representative of the great majority to whom the word of the Lord comes. Earthly things engross the mind to the exclusion of the things which belong to our peace. The Lord is anxious to reveal Himself to us, but any trifle suffices to turn us away from listening to His voice. Yet He does not become discouraged. If the Lord had nothing of special value for us,

He might be tempted to abandon the effort to gain our attention, but because that which He offers is beyond price, more than has entered into the heart of man to conceive, He cannot, for our sakes, withdraw the gift. If only we knew its worth, there would not be another moment's hesitation on our part to enter into the enjoyment of it.

Christ said to the woman of Samaria, "If thou knewest the gift of God, and Who it is that saith to thee, Give Me to drink; thou wouldest have asked of Him, and He would have given thee living water." Notice how Christ speaks of these steps as a matter of course, admitting of no question. If the woman knew what the gift of God was, she would of course, ask for it. Every one can believe that. But it is just as much a matter of course that He should grant her request. Let us remember, as we study what the living water is, and desire to drink deeply of it for ourselves, that the Lord reckons on our asking for it, and says that just as surely as we do, we shall have it. It is as natural on His part to give the water of life as it is for us to desire it, and even more so, for He gives more, exceeding abundantly more, than we can ask or even think. Eph. 3:20.

"Whosoever drinketh of the water that I shall give him shall never thirst; but the water that I shall give him shall be in him a well of water springing up into everlasting life." Here is perfect satisfaction, fullness of life, an unending rejoicing, an everlasting salvation. How little we have appreciated what Christ wants to do for His followers, the wonderful life that He desires them to live. It is not His will that there shall be any unsatisfied longings among His people, or vain hungering and thirsting after unattainable blessings. "Blessed are they which do hunger and thirst after righteousness, *for they shall be filled.*" Matt. 5:6. The blessing that Moses pronounced upon Naphtali is to be the experience of all God's children, "satisfied with favour, and full with the blessing of the Lord." Deut. 33:23. Jesus says, "I am the bread of life: he that cometh to Me shall never hunger; and He that believeth on Me shall never thirst." John 6:35.

In the earth made new there will be "a pure river of water of life, clear as crystal, proceeding out of the throne of God and of the Lamb." Rev. 22:1. This flows from God's own being for He is "the Fountain of living waters." The tree of life, which is on either side of the river, derives its exhaustless vitality from the river of life. It will be a good thing to drink of that river. Poets have sung of it, and wherever the thought of it has found an entrance into human hearts, it has awakened a thirsting which nothing else can satisfy. Whoever drinks of that stream shall find freedom from all evil, fullness of joy and pleasures forevermore. There are none who would refuse to quench their thirst with its crystal waters if they only had the chance. It is the outpouring of God's own life, and eternity and heaven are in its flow. It is written of the redeemed, "They shall hunger no more, neither thirst any more; ... for the Lamb which is in the midst of the throne shall feed them, and shall lead them into living fountains of waters: and God shall wipe away all tears from their eyes." Rev. 7:17.

We are not told of these things that we may decide to strive to win them. So far as they lie beyond the utmost stretch of the imagination, do they rise beyond the compass of human effort. Not as dazzling glimpses of the uncertain future, but as present realities, to be received and enjoyed, they are made known to us. "For all things are yours... things present or things to come." 1 Cor. 3:21, 22. "The heavenly gift" is something to be tasted now, and "the powers of the world to come" are for the present life. Heb. 6:4, 5. "Let him that is athirst come. And whosoever will, let him take the water of life freely." Rev. 22:17. To men living on this earth, even to us, Jesus says, "If any man thirst, let him come unto Me, and drink."

To drink of the living water is to drink of God's own life. What a wonderful possibility for men! It is our privilege to be filled with God's life, and to receive it as easily and naturally as we receive water when we are thirsty. His life is in all His gifts, so that as we quench our bodily thirst with pure water, we are drinking in His life. But there are so many other things for which we thirst, besides that which satisfies our physical appetites. All longing desire, ambition, discontent, lawful and unlawful, are the thirst of the soul, and nothing will quench this thirst but Christ. "He that believeth on Me shall never thirst."

Do not think that because you are unworthy it would be presumptuous on your part to come and drink. The presumption consists in not drinking. It is that of which the Lord complains. Therefore do not hesitate to accept the invitation to take of the water of life freely. "Be astonished, O ye heavens at this... saith the Lord. For My people have committed two evils; they have forsaken Me, the Fountain of livings waters, and hewed them out cisterns, broken cisterns, that can hold no water." Jer. 2:12, 13.

We need never be afraid that any privilege which the Scriptures set forth is too good for us, being reserved for some more deserving class. God's ambition for each of us is a boundless one, and He thirsts to see it realized. He is not content that men shall live far from Him, where only the little, trickling streamlets of His blessing reach them. He wants them to live at the Fountain-head, where there is always abundance. It was to secure this object that Christ came to this earth. Men had wandered away from God, every one to his own way, and Christ came to show us what it meant to live at the Fountain. "We behold His glory, the glory as of the only begotten of the Father, full of grace and truth." He Himself drank of the Fountain of life; it was the Father's life alone that was revealed in Him, and having thus shown us how desirable it is, He invites us to receive it also.

"But we are sinful and far from God," we say. That is no obstacle. "Ye who sometimes were far off are made nigh by the blood of Christ." Eph. 2:13. The Fountain that has been opened is for sin and for uncleanness. Zech. 13:1. The sin was in forsaking the Fountain. "In returning and rest shall ye be saved." There is salvation in returning to God because He Himself is our salvation. There is nothing incomplete or ineffective about the salvation. It is as perfect as God Himself, for it is Himself. Therefore God's gift to us is Himself. We draw our supplies from His being. When that stream is exhausted we may come to want, but not before. His resources are our resources. God is the strength of our life. He is our song. He is "the deep, sweet well of love." Therefore with joy will we draw water out of the wells of salvation. Isa. 12:2, 3. There is more than enough for us and for every one we desire to help. We may draw and draw, and always with joy, because there is no disappointment with the Lord. "Great is the Holy One of Israel in the midst of thee."

"And the Lord shall guide thee continually, and satisfy thy soul in drought, and make fat thy bones; and thou shalt be like a watered garden, and like a spring of water, whose waters fail not." Isa. 58:11. "They shall be abundantly satisfied with the fatness of Thy house; and Thou shalt make them drink of the river of Thy pleasures. For with Thee is the fountain of life." Ps. 36:8, 9. Only those who drink of Christ now, and find cleansing from sin in the fountain of His life, will be able to drink of the river that proceeds from the throne. Those who have no desire to drink of it now, will not care to do so then. It is God's presence that constitutes the glory and the attraction of heaven, and Christ is the brightness of His glory. That glory is given freely to us in Christ (John 17:22), and so receiving Him, we are delivered from the power of darkness and translated into the kingdom of God's dear Son. The powers of the world to come work in us, and make us meet to be partakers of the inheritance of the saints in light. Col. 1:12, 13. Unless we thus drink of Christ now, and find Him good, we should be out of harmony with the spirit and surroundings of heaven. We have the privilege now of testing the joys of the redeemed, and deciding whether we will share them or not. Those who reject them in this life do so forever. Men will not be able to accuse the Lord of unfair treatment concealing from them how desirable heaven was. None will be able to say, "Had we known how pleasant it is, we would have chosen very differently," for that which makes heaven desirable is offered to men on earth in Jesus Christ. Even here they may know what it is to thirst no more.

"He that believeth on Me, as the scripture hath said, out of his belly shall flow rivers of living water. But this spake He of the Spirit, which they that believe on Him should receive." John 7:38, 39. God imparts Himself by His Spirit, and by it dwells in mortal flesh. Those whose inner man is strengthened with it, receive Christ into their hearts and are filled with all the fullness of God. Eph. 3:16–19. Thus the Fountain of life is in them and flows forth in streams of blessing, rivers of living water. Christ was filled with the Spirit and the rivers of living water flowed from Him on earth, just as really as they flow from Him in heaven. Thus He caused the woman of Samaria to drink of the water of life, that she might thirst no more.

There is a lesson for all who labour with Christ in His experience on this occasion. No one can allow living waters to flow through him for the salvation of others without being refreshed and strengthened himself. "He that watereth shall be watered also himself." Prov. 11:25. This was true in Christ's case. When He began to talk to the woman He was hungry and weary, but in ministering to her need, He was refreshed and strengthened, so that when His disciples returned and urged Him, "Master, eat," He could say, "I have meat to eat that ye know not of." They supposed that some one must have brought Him food, but it was His meat to do His Father's will. God does not call men to exhaust themselves in His service, but to drink of the Fountain of life, and glorify Him by letting the life-giving stream flow through them, watering their own souls and making fat their bones, in lives of blessing and willing service for others.

—January 19, 1899

Chapter 6
Healing the Nobleman's Son

John 4:43–54

To us who read in the gospels the thrilling narrative of Christ's work on earth, it seems strange that any of those who knew Him in the flesh could have been so blind and deaf as to give rise to His complaint that "a prophet hath no honour in his own country." Yet in this respect Christ shared the experience of those who had in past ages given the Word of God to the people. It is true that the Jews in His day had a great respect for the prophets of bygone years. They believed that these were sent by God and that their fathers had done wrong in killing them. Said they, "If we had been in the days of our fathers, we would not have been partakers with them in the blood of the prophets." Yet when the message of God came to themselves they rejected One who was more than a prophet, and thereby showed that they were no better than their fathers.

The man in whose mouth God puts His own words always has a living message for the people, a present truth. He does not present issues which were vital in years past, but are now no longer so. His message fits the need of the hour and calls, not for approval of something that was done a hundred years ago, but for present decision. This is why a prophet has no honour in his own country. When there is no longer any risk of endangering their interests, the multitude will endorse the message and honour the prophet. In so doing they flatter themselves that they are one with the heroic souls who jeopardized their lives by obeying the truth when it was unpopular. Satan is well content that men shall adopt truths which were vital in past generations, if he can thus obscure truth which has a special application at the present time.

In His words to the Jewish nobleman Christ struck at the difficulty which made it possible for His own countrymen to reject Him. "Except ye see signs and wonders ye will not believe." Men do not see anything remarkable in that to which they are accustomed. The early years of Jesus had been largely spent at Nazareth, and there His blameless life had revealed the glory of God, yet His fellow townsmen saw nothing in Him to justify the assertion that He was anointed by God for the special work. "And they said, Is not this Joseph's son?" as if that were of itself sufficient to overthrow His claim.

Jesus Himself was a most wonderful sign, but His neighbours saw nothing extraordinary in Him. They thought that if He would give them a sign such as Moses or Elijah gave, they would believe. Really, their thought was, Convince every one that you are the Messiah, and when we see everybody else recognizing you, we will do so also. They did not wish to incur the odium of espousing an unpopular cause. They wanted Him first to get rid of the reproach, and since none of the mighty works which He wrought effected this, none of them answered the purpose of the sign which they desired.

For all whose hearts were open to receive light and truth Christ's own life was a sign, but it got Him no honour in His own country. It is an incomprehensible marvel that God speaks to us in His own Word, yet how many see any wonder in it? They say, If God would thunder His word into our ears as He did at Sinai, we would believe it. It is a wonderful work that God does in providing us with food and drink, with air and light, by the unceasing exercise of His power and wisdom, yet men see nothing worthy of notice in it. They say that if God would rain bread from heaven as He did on Israel, or turn water into wine as He did at Cana of Galilee, they would no longer doubt Him. The miracles which God daily and hourly works in the sight of men get Him no honour among those who are accustomed to His working. "The ox knoweth his owner, and the ass his master's crib, but Israel doth not know, My people doth not consider."

The nobleman, whose son was sick at Capernaum, came to Jesus very much as the majority of people come when they desire to receive something from Him. He "besought Him that He would come down, and heal his son; for he was at the point of death." His heart was full of an intense desire, and the reproof implied in the words of Jesus, "Except ye see signs and wonders ye will not believe," could not turn the father's thoughts from the boon that he sought so earnestly. His only response was, "Sir, come down ere my child die." This man did not come in strong faith, as did the centurion who asked only that the word of healing might be spoken, but Jesus does not repulse the nobleman because of his lack of faith. He is touched with the feeling of our infirmities; and His own heart responded to the father's cry for help. So when burdened hearts pour out their longing to the Lord, He inclines His ear to them, even though they know but little of true faith.

But Jesus taught the nobleman how to believe. He said, "Go thy way; thy son liveth." And the man believed the word and went his way. So many do not know what faith is. They think it is some quality possessed by themselves, of which some men have much and others little. Sometimes they say, "Yes, I believe what the Lord says, but I have not faith enough to do it." They think they can estimate the amount of faith they have, and that everything depends upon the amount. "Faith cometh by hearing, and hearing by the word of God." Faith is simply believing what God says. There is no question of how much you believe. The point is, Do you believe? What would you think if someone should say to you, "Yes, I believe what you say, but I don't believe you very much." You would conclude that the person did not believe you at all. Christ says that faith as a grain of mustard-seed will remove mountains. It is not your faith but the Word you believe that does such great things. God's Word is infinitely powerful, therefore whatever it says must be so and you believe it when it speaks. This is faith. If the Word makes a great promise, and you believe it, you have great faith. It was hearing the Word that gave the nobleman faith.

Would you like to be strong in faith? Then let the Word of God dwell in you richly. Receive it not as the word of men, but as it is in truth the Word of God; listen to it, meditate upon it, hide it in your heart, and you will be full of faith, for "faith cometh by hearing." If you listen to God speaking, the faith will come naturally, without effort on your part. When the dead hear the voice of the Son of God, they that hear shall live. Therefore, though you be dead in trespasses and sins, listen to God's Word and you will live, live by faith.

Too often when we kneel in prayer and pour out our heart before God, we rise from our knees and go our way as though nothing had been accomplished, beyond the natural relief that comes from telling our troubles. Jesus has said, "Ask, and it shall be given you; seek, and ye shall find." "Every one that asketh receiveth." "Whatsoever ye shall ask in My name, that will I do." Every one may ask whatsoever he will in the name of Christ, and know that his request is granted, for the Lord has definitely said so. Then when we pray to the Lord, we are not to rise from our knees and go our way, still troubled and anxious, but know that, since God honours His own promise, our desires are granted. The Lord gives us blank cheques in which we may insert our own name, and whatsoever we desire. If a wealthy man should give us such an opportunity as this, we should not be slow to take advantage of it, and when we had taken the cheque to the bank, and handed it to the cashier, we should not go away feeling as poor and unsatisfied as ever. We would know that we are richer than we were by the full amount of the cheque, and we may know, just as certainly, by the Lord's oft-repeated guarantee, that we are enriched to the extent that we have asked for in our prayer. It was in this assurance that the nobleman took his way home, and he learned from the servants who came to meet him that at the very hour Jesus had said, "Thy son liveth," the fever left his child.

Jesus came to reveal the Father, not to obscure His character. If the miracles wrought by Jesus were not indicative of God's continual desire to help us, Christ's course in healing so many would simply draw a veil of mystery over His Father, and leave us in perplexing doubt as to what we might expect that He would do for us. When we realize that Christ was the expression of God's good-will to men, all the circumstances of this miracle are encouraging: the reception of the father's petition, the way in which he was led to believe and the immediate results that followed the healing word, speak to us of the possibilities that await us in the Word of God when we believe it simply, and thus allow it to work.

There is a word which God has spoken to us all, which has as much of personal application and a wonder-working power, also of instantaneous performance, for us as the word spoken to the nobleman had for him and his son. The Lord says to us, "Wash you, make you clean, put away the evil of your doings from before Mine eyes." Isa. 1:16. There seems to be so little of encouragement in these words that few will question their application to themselves. It is clear that no one can be in worse condition than the people described in the first chapter of Isaiah to whom these words are addressed, so that they take in every sinner. What is the force of the command, "Put away the evil of your doings from before Mine eyes?" When Christ bade the lepers be clean it was He who supplied that which was needed. The lepers did not feel discouraged at His asking them to do an impossible thing. It was for Him to look after the impossibility. Similarly, when He bade the lame walk they rejoiced, for He found the needed power. So too when He says to us, "Put away the evil of your doings from before Mine eyes," the more impossible the thing sounds the more we are to rejoice at the great work which this word accomplishes in us. It needs Divine strength to accomplish such a task, but this strength is in the commandment. All that is needed is for us to hear and believe that the blessed command may be fulfilled in us just as the words "Come forth" were fulfilled in Lazarus.

Think how much is involved in this command. The Lord says, "Put away the evil of your doings from before Mine eyes." But there is nothing that is not naked and open to the eyes of Him with whom we have to do. Therefore to put anything out of His sight is to put it out of existence. That is, our doings are to be sinless in the Lord's eyes. We cannot possibly do this ourselves, because we have secret sins that we have not yet discovered in their true character. But these are in the sight of the Lord, and are therefore included in the command. "Thou hast set our iniquities before Thee, our secret sins in the light of Thy countenance." Ps. 90:8. These hidden springs of evil that make the heart

so desperately wicked, and deceitful above all things so that none can know it, the Lord has commanded us to remove from His sight. Shall we sigh and say it is impossible, or believe the Word and in its strength obey? It is God who gives the command, and when we believe His word of power we may rejoice that it works effectually in us who believe. Of the people who thus by faith obey the Word of God, it is written, "the iniquity of Israel shall be sought for, and there shall be none; and the sins of Judah, and they shall not be found." Jer. 50:20.
—*January 26, 1899*

Chapter 7
Man's Rightful Authority

John 5:17–27

A Miracle

Jesus had just performed a great miracle. A man who for thirty-eight years had been unable to walk, had been instantly healed, insomuch that at the command of Jesus he arose, took up the pallet on which he had been lying, and walked. "And on the same day was the Sabbath." John 5:9.

"Therefore did the Jews persecute Jesus, and sought to slay Him, because He had done these things on the Sabbath day." Verse 16. Of course Jesus well knew that they would do this. Why then did He perform that special miracle on the Sabbath day? The man was not in imminent danger. After thirty-eight years of waiting, one more day would not have been so intolerable. For that matter, Jesus might doubtless have done the deed the day before as well as not; for the man had been long lying by the pool, and Jesus could not have failed to see him. Did Jesus wish to irritate the Jews, and deliberately to defy their prejudices? It is impossible to harbour such a suggestion for a moment, for it is utterly foreign to His character.

True Sabbath Observance

Why, then, was this miracle of healing, like so many others that are expressly mentioned, performed on the Sabbath day?—Because Jesus would show the true object and meaning of the Sabbath. He would show that it is *for* man, and not against him,—that it is not a burdensome yoke, but a lifter of burdens. He would teach us that the Sabbath, as the memorial of God's perfect and complete work, makes known the measure of God's power to make both soul and body "every whit whole."

When the Jews persecuted Jesus for the good deed done to the impotent man, He justified Himself by saying, "My Father worketh hitherto, and I work." That was a real justification of His act, for to do that which God does is the most perfect righteousness. Moreover, the acts of Jesus were not simply copies of what the Father did; if they were, then there would be in them no lessons or help for us, for it would show no connection between Him and frail human beings. But He said, "I do nothing of Myself;" "but the Father that dwelleth in Me, He doeth the works." John 8:28; 14:10. There is no man so weak that he cannot let God work in him to will and to do of His good pleasure.

Jesus was accused of violating the Sabbath, and He did indeed break the Jewish Sabbath, but not the Sabbath of the Lord. The Jewish Sabbath consisted in formal cessation of all labour on the seventh day of the week, even though human life was lost thereby. It was simply a yoke, a burden, an act of penance, by which they thought to make themselves righteous. It had nothing in common with the Sabbath of the Lord except that it was kept on the same day of the week. The Lord's Sabbath is absolute rest in Him and His word,—dependence on His life; and since His life is activity,—service to others,—it follows that true Sabbath-keeping may sometimes involve severe physical labour. How can one tell what works are lawful on the Sabbath day, and what are not?—No list of lawful and unlawful works can be given, but this principle will guide: whatever labour is necessary for the welfare of suffering humanity, whether the disease be of the body or of soul, and from which the labourer derives absolutely no profit or benefit except the consciousness of God's presence, is proper Sabbath labour. True Sabbath-keeping is rest in God,—absolute and unqualified acceptance of His word.

"My father worketh hitherto, and I work." How does God work, and how had Jesus done the work for which He was now persecuted?—By His word. Mark this: It was not as a man works by giving orders to another. No man may flatter himself that he is keeping the Sabbath while others are labouring in his employ. Whosoever does a thing by another does it himself. It is not the way that God works, and it was not in that way that Jesus healed the impotent man. He did not speak the word which set somebody else to work, but *His word itself did the work.* "By the word of the Lord were the heavens made, and all the host of them by the breath of His mouth." "He spake, and it was." Ps. 33:6, 9. This miracle of Jesus was therefore simply a manifestation of the creative power of God's word.

In six days God created the heavens and the earth; and then He rested on the seventh day, not because to have continued the work of creation would have been a sin, but for the good reason that it was all done. The word, however, continued to work in upholding that which it had created. All the works of God since that time (so far at least as this earth is concerned) are simply to uphold or to restore, and the works which He does for us and through us are to the same effect. Keeping the Sabbath of the Lord is simply the absolute resting in God's finished work, and allowing Him to put them into us. The absolute ceasing from all our own works on the seventh day,—from everything by which we may get gain,—is an indication of our trust in God for "life, and breath, and all things." If one dare not trust God to keep him if he should rest on what is to all the world (and even the greater part of the professed Christian world,) the busiest day of the week, how can he persuade himself that he is trusting God for eternity?

Right and Authority of a Son

"The Son can do nothing of Himself, but what He seeth the Father do; for what things soever the Father doeth, these also doeth the Son likewise. For the Father loveth the Son, and showeth Him all things that Himself doeth; and He will show Him greater works than these, that ye may marvel. For as the Father raiseth up the dead, and quickeneth them; even so the Son quickeneth whom He will. For the Father judgeth no man, but hath committed all judgment unto the Son; that all men should honour the Son even as they honour the Father." John 5:19–23.

Every son is necessarily the heir of his father. Legislation, knavery, the caprice of the father, or something else, may exclude a son from any share in the father's property; but nothing can deprive any child that is born into the world of his essential heirship, namely, the parents' individual characteristics. The father bestows himself, whatever he may be, upon his son, and this is the son's essential heirship. Even so Christ is "the image of the invisible God" (Col. 1:15), "the brightness of His glory." Heb. 1:3. Humanity is imperfect, and can therefore only imperfectly reproduce itself, so that a son may be vastly inferior to his father in many or in all respects; but God, whose every way is perfect, reveals every perfection of His character in His Son—"the Beginning of His way." Therefore the only-begotten Son has by birthright the power and authority of the Father. Therefore it is that all judgment is committed to Him. To Him it is given to rule the nations, and at the last to break them in pieces like a potter's vessel; but this power is not arbitrarily bestowed; it is simply one phase of the working of the "power over all flesh" which Christ has in Himself, and which He uses for the salvation of mankind.

"For as the Father hath life in Himself, so hath He given to the Son to have life in Himself; and hath given Him authority to execute judgment also; because He is the Son of man." John 5:26, 27. How different that is from what we would have written. We would have said that the Father hath given the Son authority to execute judgment, because He is the Son of God; but no;

the reason is that He is the Son of man. This brings us face to face with the rightful place of man on this earth.

By virtue of the first creation, man is the son of God. Luke 3:38. As such authority over all the earth was given him. Remember that the authority was given him in creation. He was made a king. The authority was in him. Just as the magnet is not a magnet because men agree to call it so, but because it has in itself drawing power, so man was king by virtue of what was in him, namely, the life of God. He had dominion over the beasts, the birds, the fishes, and over the earth itself. These did not obey Him because they had agreed to, or were told to, but because he had the authority that they could not help recognizing and yielding to. Everything was placed in subjection to man, and remained so as long as man was in subjection to God.

Man's first dominion was one of glory, for he was "crowned with glory and honour" when he was placed over the works of God's hands. Heb. 2:7. But "all have sinned, and come short of the glory of God." Rom. 2:23. Consequently the dominion has been lost. Man is no longer king by nature, because he does not have kingly power in him. Now comes Christ in human flesh, made in all things like unto His brethren (Heb. 2:17), tasting death for every man, and crowned with glory and honour. He "was made of the seed of David according to the flesh, and declared to be the Son of God with power, according to the Spirit of holiness, by the resurrection from the dead." Rom. 1:3, 4. So through Jesus the dominion of the earth still remains in the hands of man; for it must be remembered that Jesus came to earth as man, to win back the dominion for man. God never lost the dominion, or any part of it. Christ did not need to come to earth to get the dominion of the earth, and authority to execute judgment, for Himself as God, for that He had; but it was that the dominion given to man might be perpetuated. Therefore it is that Christ was on earth as man in every respect. He represented God to man, that God might in Him exhibit His idea of a man.

The one who rules is the one to judge. Man is rightful lord of this earth, and therefore he is the one to whom judgment is necessarily committed. "The saints shall judge the world." 1 Cor. 6:2. "Let the saints be joyful in glory; let them sing aloud upon their beds. Let the high praises of God be in their mouth, and a two-edged sword in their hand; to execute vengeance upon the heathen, and punishments upon the people; to bind their kings with chains, and their nobles with fetters of iron; to execute upon them the judgment written; this honour have all His saints." Ps. 149:5–9. But they have this power only when as sons of men they are also sons of God. In Christ, through the eternal Spirit, we become the sons of God as surely as we are now the sons of our parents, and are heirs of His goodness as surely as we by nature inherit the traits of our earthly fathers. Through the exceeding great and precious promises of God we become "partakers of the Divine nature." 2 Peter 1:4. "As many as received Him, to them gave He power to become the sons of God, even to them that believe on His name. Which were born, not of blood, nor of the will of the flesh, nor of the will of man, but of God." John 1:12, 13. Thus are we joint-heirs with Jesus Christ, having rights and privileges with Him. In Him we become "one new man," created in the Divine image.

And now that we see it for a fact that "as He is so are we in this world" (1 John 4:17), we may grasp something of the significance of the wonderful works that He did. Remember that Christ, the Son of God, became the Son of man, in order that we, the sons of men, might become the sons of God. He was made in all things like unto us, that we might become in all things like unto Him. Now read again:

"Verily, verily, I say unto you, the Son can do nothing of Himself, but what He seeth the Father do; for what things soever He doeth, these also doeth the Son likewise. For the Father loveth the Son, and showeth Him all things that Himself doeth; and He will show Him greater works than these, that ye may marvel." John 5:19, 20.

What does this mean to us?—Everything. It is a part of our inheritance. If we are "in Him," sons of God through faith in Christ Jesus, called by His name, and walking worthy of the calling, then as joint heirs with Him, sharers of His glory and dominion, we may know that all this applies to us the same as to Jesus of Nazareth. "But we are so weak and helpless," you say. Very well, it is impossible to be more helpless than to be able to do nothing of one's own self. See verses 19, 30. Jesus does the thing that He sees the Father do, not by Himself as a copyist, but by the Father dwelling in Him. To us He says, "All things that I have heard of My Father I have made known to you" (John 15:15), and "He that believeth in Me, the works that I do shall he do also." John 14:12. Don't take counsel of past experience, and say that it is too much to believe, and impossible, but take counsel of the Spirit, who alone makes known the riches of the glory of the inheritance.

Jesus of Nazareth was "a man approved of God" "by miracles and wonders and signs which God did by Him." Acts. 2:22. Wondrous things He did for men, and even greater works were to be done. So to us He says that, believing, we shall do the works that He did, and greater also. What an unspeakable gift! What an incentive to yield ourselves to Him, to be perfectly cleansed from all taint of the curse, and made "complete in Him," "a perfect man," even up to "the measure of the stature of the fullness of Christ." What! poor fallen mortals to have power to heal the sick and the lame, and to cast out devils with a word? Even so, for so it is written, and so it shall be, even as it has already been. Not one only, but every believer in Christ, must have this authority. Don't try to understand it, but believe it and accept it; for what the eye hath not seen, nor the ear heard, and what have not entered into the heart of man, namely the things which God hath prepared for those that love Him,—those things hath God revealed unto us by His Holy Spirit; for the Spirit searcheth all things, even the deep things of God, and is freely bestowed on us that we may know the things that are freely given to us of God. "Thanks be unto God for His unspeakable gift."

—February 2, 1899

Chapter 8
Christian Giving

John 6:1–12

Jesus had gone across the sea of Galilee, and as was usually the case whenever He went anywhere, "a great multitude followed Him." Why was it that people flocked in such numbers around this poor man—a man so poor that He had no home, no place where He could lay His head?—It was because He had something to give which they wanted. It was not food or money, although even in His poverty He did give those things; but such gifts were only secondary; the people could work and earn money, and buy bread, but He gave them freely that which money could not buy. They followed Him "because they saw His miracles which He did on them that were diseased." He had a message of power, words of life,—and people were drawn to Him by an attraction which they could not understand or explain.

When Jesus saw the multitude around Him as He taught (for there were not fewer than five thousand men, besides women and children), He said to Philip, but in the hearing of all the disciples, "Whence shall we buy bread, that these may eat?" Philip made a hasty calculation, and said; "Two hundred pennyworth of bread is not sufficient for them, that every one of them may take a little." Remember that the purchasing power of money was very different then from what it is now. A penny was the ordinary wage for a day's labour. See Matt. 20:1, 2. Two pence was a good deposit toward the lodging and care of an invalid at an inn. See Luke 10:30–35. Two hundred pence would therefore buy a great quantity of bread, yet not enough so that each one of the company could have just a taste, and Philip could see no way of helping the hungry crowd.

It was very evident to the disciples that no matter how great the need of the company, and how disposed they themselves were to assist them, the thing could not be done. So they said to Jesus, "Send the multitude away, that they may go into the villages, and buy themselves victuals." Matt. 14:15. But even if this were done, many must have gone hungry, having no money to buy with. "Jesus said unto them, They need not depart; give ye them to eat."

Again the business sense of the disciples was brought into requisition, and they looked over their resources, and found so meager a supply that it was useless to speak about it. Peter, acting as a spokesman for the twelve, said, "There is a lad here which hath five barley loaves, and two small fishes; but what are they among so many?" Clearly nothing could be done. "Oh, no; it is useless to talk; we should like to feed these hungry people, but we have nothing worth mentioning to do it with; we have carefully considered the situation, and it is absolutely impossible to do anything. Oh, if we only had means!"

All this time Jesus "Himself knew what He would do." The business calculations of the disciples, and the demonstration that they were in too straitened circumstances to allow of their doing anything to help, did not effect Him in the least. He was not discouraged at the prospect. Five loaves and two fishes? Oh, that is an abundance! "Make the men sit down." Everything must be orderly. We don't want any pushing and crowding, any unseemly scramble for the overflow of food that is to be provided. There must be no chance for some weak, timid person to be overlooked. Moreover there must be quiet, so that all can have opportunity to think upon the wondrous gift of God, and upon the Giver. Let the men be still, that they may recognize God. So the men sat down, "and Jesus took the loaves; and when He had given thanks, He distributed to the disciples, and the disciples to them that were set down; and likewise of the fishes as much as they would. When they were filled, He said unto His disciples, Gather up the fragments that remain, that nothing be lost. Therefore they gathered them together, and filled twelve baskets with the fragments of the five barley loaves which remained over and above unto them that had eaten."

Here is the story complete; only a few of the lessons that it teaches can be noted at present. For the first we may see the tender compassion of Jesus on the poor and needy. His heart was and is always touched by the sight of human need and suffering. Everything moves Him. He is "touched with the feeling of our infirmities." But He doesn't rest content with mere pity and expressions of sympathy. He wastes no time in regrets that He is not able to help; but from His abundant fullness He supplies the want. His sympathy is practical, and always accomplishes something. He sympathizes; He longs to do something to help; He knows what He will do; and He does it. He knows the need; He cares for it; and He is able and willing to relieve.

The Lord allows us to realize our helplessness. His question, "Whence shall we buy bread, that these may eat?" was calculated to emphasize the great need and their lack of means. But remember that the question was not one of doubt. "He Himself knew what He would do." Let this case, then, stand as the type of all. How often we have felt our hearts stirred as we have seen poverty and suffering, and have longed to help, and have mourned our inability. Now that desperate situation, that was made so vivid to us, was only the repetition of the Lord's question to Philip, Whence shall we supply these hungry souls with food? And just as the question was asked then to prove the disciples, so the desperate need is set before us so vividly in order to prove us. How often we have been tested in this manner, and yet we have not learned the lesson. May we begin now.

Jesus would not send people away hungry. He would not allow the disciples to do so. He always feeds the hungry. Therefore we may be assure that when we allow people to go away hungry for food either for the body or the soul, we ignore or deny the presence of the Master among us. "He that saith he abideth in Him ought himself also so to walk even as He walked." 1 John 2:6. "Verily, verily, I say unto you, He that believeth on Me, the works that I do shall he do also; and greater works than these shall he do; because I go unto the Father." John 14:12.

"They need not depart; give ye them to eat." Why did Jesus say that?—Because it was so. Jesus did not trifle with the disciples. He knew what *He* would do; the question was, Did they know what *they* would do? Yes; they knew that they would send the multitude away empty; but they did not need to. His question to Philip was for the purpose of proving him, and the rest of the disciples as well. The words of Jesus show that if they had but recognized their opportunity they might have fed the multitude the same as He did. And the lesson is recorded for our sakes.

"How can we give when we have nothing?"—Just the same as Jesus did when He had nothing; for He did not do anything while here on this earth, except as *man*.

"Yes; but it pleased the Father that in Him all fullness should dwell, and it was of the abundant fullness that was in Him, that He fed the multitudes." Very true; "and of His fullness have all we received." John 1:16. The same Christ is alive today, and dwells among us; and if we but allow Him to dwell in our hearts *by faith*, we shall also "be filled with all the fullness of God." Eph. 3:19.

What a marvelous manifestation of the power of God's grace! that having nothing we should be able to give everything. "We then as workers together with Him beseech you that ye receive not the grace of God in vain;" and we approve ourselves as the ministers of God, "as poor, yet making many rich; as having nothing, and yet possessing all things." 2 Cor. 6:1, 10.

Peter and John found a man at the gate of the temple in sore need. He asked for money, but Peter had none to give him. This did not, however, make it necessary for Peter to pass by with a sympathetic greeting and a remark,

Christian Giving

"Poor fellow! how I wish I could do something for him." No; Peter gave the man something better than money,—something that money could not buy, but that which would enable him to get money if he needed it. When all God's professed people have Christ's abiding presence through the Holy Spirit, as a reality of which they are conscious, they will never pass a needy soul by without supplying more than he asks or thinks to receive.

God gives us richly all things to enjoy. "He giveth to all life, and breath, and all things." Acts 17:25. Everybody therefore has everything given to him. Most people, however, do not recognize the gifts of God. Not only do they not know God as the Giver of every good and perfect gift, but they do not know how abundantly He gives, even when they know that He does give something. It is the business of God's servants, therefore, "to open the blind eyes" (Isa. 42:7), that men may know the boundless grace of God, and the gift by grace. They are to be "good stewards of the manifold grace of God." 1 Peter 4:10. But oh, how sad it is when those who profess to know God are themselves blind to the riches of the glory of their inheritance. Who is there of us who has not discounted the words of Jesus, and the lessons that He has left us, so much that they have scarcely any more meaning to us than as mere stories? Shall we not learn?

As we have freely received, so are we freely to give. That is, we are to give as much as we have received, and on the same terms. We have received everything; we are to give everything. The fact that we do not have a big stock to carry about with us to exhibit, does not prove that we have nothing. God is our treasure house. "The unsearchable riches of Christ" are all and always "in Him," for "in Him are al things created," and "in Him all things consist," and He is ours. He saves us the trouble of looking after and caring for our vast property, while we have all the use of it on demand. He says, "Concerning the work of My hands, command ye Me." Isa. 45:11. These are realities, and not empty words.

In all this God is trying to teach the world that "a man's life consisteth not in the abundance of the things which he possesseth" or seemeth to have. He would have us know, and teach others, that He cares for us, and keeps us. He would have all men know that all things come from Him, so that all may give Him glory, by receiving from Him the things that He gives. True, He has said that the man who will not work shall not eat, but that does not teach us that man must support himself. No man on earth "earns his own living." No man can earn a living. Life is too precious a commodity to be bought with money, or earned by human labour. Life is a gift. God "*giveth* to all life, and breath, and all things." The occasions when He gives us help, when it is manifest that we are unable to do anything for ourselves, are to show us that even where we are most active we simply gather up what He showers down.

Now when Christ's followers rise to their privileges as "workers together with Him," realizing that He was on earth as a representative Man, showing what every child of God ought to do when occasion calls for it, the world will see that there is something better than what this world can give. They will not all believe, but the work that God designs for the world will speedily be accomplished. They will see that poverty does not handicap a man of God; that the expression "rich in faith" is not an empty phrase; and that the poor Christian can do what the wealthy worldling cannot. How to give with nothing is the lesson that God teaches, for He takes the things that are not, when He has a great work to do.

Therefore let us know that a great need only magnifies God's gift. Instead of despairing when we cannot see the way to accomplish a necessary thing, remember that Christ Himself is the way. Yea, He is a "new and living way." With Him at hand, knowing His real presence, we do not need to be worried over "ways and means." When the Lord asked Philip how they could buy bread for the multitude, Philip might well have answered, "Lord, Thou knowest, for Thou art the Bread."

Christ "gave Himself for us," and the reality of the gift is demonstrated in the feeding of the multitude, for He literally gave Himself to them. But as He Himself said, He could do nothing of Himself. It was the Father dwelling in Him who did the works. He comes to dwell in believers, that they may be filled with the fullness of God, so that they may also do the same as He did. We see that the disciples did give the people bread, after all. They took it from Jesus, and gave it to the multitude. That is to show us that we may feed the hungry when we are in touch with Him. Let each servant of Christ take the bread of life fresh from Him, and pass it on.

As Christ gave Himself, so are we to give ourselves. This we can really do when we can say, "I am crucified with Christ, nevertheless I live; yet not I, but Christ liveth in me." Gal. 2:20. He who does not give himself gives nothing, even though he bestows thousands of gold and silver. He who gives himself (and he can do it only by the grace of Christ dwelling in him), gives everything that any soul can need, even though he has not a penny.

What will then follow?—The same thing that took place with Jesus. Multitudes ran after Him, because He gave them Himself. So "thou shalt call a nation that thou knowest not, and nations that knew not thee shall run unto thee because of the Lord thy God, and for the Holy One of Israel; for He hath glorified thee." Isa. 55:5. If He has glorified thee, then "the Gentiles shall come to thy light, and kings to the brightness of thy rising." Isa. 55:3.

All will receive abundantly, but there will be no waste. Doubtless there were many "unworthy" persons in the crowd that day. He fed them all; for He was the Son of the Highest, who "maketh His sun to rise on the evil and on the good, and sendeth rain on the just and unjust." Matt. 5:45. He even causes it to "rain on the earth where no man is; in the wilderness, wherein there is no man." Job 38:26. The ocean also, where there is no need of water, receives showers equally with the dry land. So lavish is God with His gifts. Yet there is no waste; for He draweth again all the drops of water to Himself. He gathers up the fragments so that nothing is lost. All comes back to Him, to be again given forth. What if the recipient be unworthy? Know that God does not ask you to give because He needs your help to supply the needy, but that you may be blessed in giving. If it were simply to see that somebody's wants were supplied, God could do that without your appearance on the scene. He allows you to share His work, that you may be partaker of His riches and joy; and this is accomplished for you, no matter what be the character of the one helped. So to him that gives shall there be given. That which he imparts, namely the life of God, will come back to him again, to make him doubly rich. Thus may we be channels for the great stream of life that flows from God throughout all the universe, and returning to His bosom flows forth again ever fresh and new.

—February 9, 1899

Chapter 9
Living by the Father

John 7:28–37

The life of Jesus, as recorded in the Gospels, sets forth not merely the pattern life for all men, but also the means by which the same life may be reproduced in whoever desires to live it. The Saviour, it is true, lived and worked and spake as never man had done before, but this was not because of any special advantages enjoyed by Him. His life was lived on earth to show what could be done with the opportunities provided by God for all men. He was poor, having nowhere to lay His head, He was despised and rejected of men, neither did His brethren believe on Him. He was tempted in all points like as we are, and counted unworthy to live by those who thought themselves righteous. Whatever of disability and hindrance is felt by any man, was Christ's portion. "His visage was so marred more than any man, and His form more than the sons of men."

There was one thing, however, that enabled Jesus to rise above His surroundings, and live a life that showed to men "the glory as of the only begotten of the Father, full of grace and truth." He represented the Father perfectly, so that He could say, "He that hath seen Me hath seen the Father," and that which enabled Him to do this was the fact that the Father dwelt in Him. Jesus emptied Himself, and interposed no obstacle to the Father's working in Him, and since God giveth not the Spirit by measure, it followed naturally that in Christ dwelt all the fullness of the Godhead bodily.

God desires to do for us what He did for His only begotten Son. Jesus said to His disciples, "As the Father hath sent Me, even so send I you." John 20:21. By pursuing the same course that Jesus took, the same results will follow in our case. So far as God is concerned, no difference is made between us and Christ. Just as He equipped and sent forth Jesus, He sends us also. Jesus recognized what the Father was to Him in all His life, and so we do not find Him thinking, planning, speaking, acting, or claiming anything for Himself, but leaving all things to His Father. "I am not come of Myself," He said, "I am come in My Father's name." Although Christ has sent us forth, just as He Himself was sent, we, instead of committing everything to God, take matters into our own hands. We are afraid that if we did not, sometimes at least, take the initiative, nothing would be done. Others expect us to take action, and although we cannot see what is the best thing to do we feel that something must be done. Saul, after waiting the appointed time for Samuel, thought it was incumbent on him to offer the sacrifice himself but he was told that he had done foolishly. 1 Sam. 13. The Lord bids us to trust in Him with all the heart, and not even to lean to our own understanding. Prov. 3:5. "Commit thy way unto the Lord; trust also in Him; and He shall bring it to pass." Ps. 37:5.

Christ was dependent on His Father through every step of His life. If God had not given Him the word to speak, it would never have been spoken, for He had none of Himself. If God had not revealed to Him the course to take, nothing would have been done, for He came not to do His own will. Christ "emptied Himself" and if the Father had not filled Him, He would have remained empty. If we confess our own helplessness and emptiness, and wait on the Lord at all times, is there any danger that our life record will be a barren one? It was not so with Christ. If we find ourselves in some situation where it might seem that we should speak, and the Lord gives us no word to speak, we are not to conclude that the Lord has overlooked us and decide to take the matter into our own hands, but know that the Lord has nothing for us to say, and that, at that time, silence is golden. Jesus was brought into circumstances where to human eyes, it would seem that every consideration demanded instant and energetic speech, but the Father gave Him nothing to say, and so He answered never a word. So He says to those whom He sends forth, "It is not ye that speak, but the Spirit of your Father which speaketh in you." Matt. 10:19, 20.

Jesus had such confidence in His Father that He could wait for Him to give the right word or act, and the Father was never found wanting. He never disappointed His Son, and He never will disappoint those who commit their way to Him, leaving Him to will and to do of His own good pleasure, and who are prepared never to speak another word or perform another act which does not originate with Him. "They shall not be ashamed that wait for Me." Isa. 49:23.

Men were surprised at the learning of Jesus. He had not attended the schools of the rabbis, yet He spoke with authority, and all recognized the unanswerable wisdom of His utterances. The explanation was, "My teaching is not Mine, but His that sent Me." He had not learned of an earthly teacher. The Father Himself was teaching through Christ, and as Elihu asked, "Who is a teacher like unto Him?"

The works of Christ did not proceed from Himself. "The Father that dwelleth in Me, He doeth the works." Yet none could deny that His life was filled with good works. The Jews said, "When Christ cometh, will He do more miracles than these which this man hath done?" So with the words of Christ. He said, "The words that I speak unto you I speak not of Myself," yet Gentile soldiers were forced to confess, "Never man spake like this Man."

Christ's qualification for the work of revealing the Father, consisted in the fact that there was nothing in Him that was not of the Father. Since He lived by the Father, and there was nothing in His life that came from any other source, every thought and word and action was a revelation of God's way. It is to be the same with all Christ's followers. "If any man be in Christ, he is a new creature: old things are passed away; behold, all things are become new. And all things are of God." 2 Cor. 5:17, 18. It is not possible for Christians to regard this matter with indifference. No one may excuse himself by saying that the standard is too high for anyone to live up to, and no one may think that he will reserve to himself the privilege of thinking his own thoughts and speaking his own words occasionally. Christ draws a sharp line of distinction between those who deny themselves, take up their cross daily, and follow Him, and those who love the praise of men and esteem anything above their Lord. He says, "He that speaketh from himself seeketh his own glory." John 7:18. Whoever seeks his own glory cannot receive Christ, for He is meek and lowly in heart. It was for this reason that the Jews could not believe on Christ, and the same difficulty in us will prove just as fatal. "How can ye believe, which receive glory one of another?" John 5:44.

In hating Christ, and seeking His life, the Jews showed what was their real feeling toward the Father. They professed themselves very jealous for the honour of Jehovah, because they thought He was altogether such an one as themselves, but when they became acquainted with His true character, as revealed in His Son, many of them hated Him without a cause. They were filled with the murderous spirit of Satan, and at the first opportunity they put the Son of God to death. Satan's spirit has not changed, and it animates all who do not allow God to think and speak in them. In seeking their own glory, they are repeating that which caused Satan's fall from heaven, and changed him from an anointed cherub to the prince of devils. While the professed church of Christ seeks its own glory, Satan can do much to further his own plans through its unconscious instrumentality, but when its members become like their Lord, and let God speak and work in them, Satan's wrath will be speedily aroused against them, and he will stir up his followers to destroy the members of Christ's body. "All that will live godly *in Christ Jesus* shall suffer persecution." All in whose hearts Christ dwells by faith may know that He by whom they live is the object of Satan's deadliest hatred, and that they themselves will share his rage, but they may know also that Christ's perfect victory over all the power of the enemy is theirs as well.

"Judge not according to appearance, but judge righteous judgment." One of the most remarkable things about Jesus was the way in which He distinguished between right and wrong. Puzzling questions were often brought to Him, but were always solved with such wisdom that those were dumbfounded. We need the same wisdom, for the traditions of men, false theories, and considerations of expediency have so confused the distinction between right and wrong in men's minds, that many honest believe wrong to be right and right to be wrong. What will clear the issues for us? The same state of things existed in Christ's day, but the prevailing mental confusion did not dim His judgment, for God Himself was His judgment. He did not judge according to appearances, for while this is all that humanity has to go by, appearances are often misleading. Jesus said, "I can of Myself do nothing: as I hear, I judge: and My judgment is righteous; because I seek not Mine own will, but the will of Him that sent Me." John 5:30. Selfish interests always cloud the judgment, and bias the decision, but Christ was swayed by none of these. Because He sought only the will of God, and listened only to His voice, the Father was to Him for " a spirit of judgment to him that sitteth in judgment." It was foretold of Christ; "The Spirit of the Lord shall rest upon Him, the spirit of wisdom and understanding, the spirit of counsel and might, the spirit of knowledge and of the fear of the Lord; and He shall be of quick understanding in the fear of the Lord: and He shall not judge after the sight of His eyes, neither decide after the hearing of His ears: but with righteousness shall He judge the poor; and reprove with equity for the meek of the earth." Isa. 11:2–4. This same Spirit is given to all freely, and will be, to all who receive it, what it was in Jesus of Nazareth.

It was never intended that the experience of Jesus, in these matters, should be an exceptional one. So far from that, God has covenanted, and the covenant is sealed with the blood of Christ, that He will put His law in our inward parts, and write it in our hearts. The Father's will was in the heart of the Son; and He delighted to do it. Ps. 90:8. God does everything in perfect righteousness because that is the law of His being, and that same law He puts into our hearts. It is perfectly natural for Him to do right, and it will be the same for those who let Him write His law in their hearts. They will judge righteous judgment, will speak words in season, and always do the right thing in the right way, because God's way is in their hearts. God Himself is their life. They, like Christ, do not need that any man teach them, for the covenant is, "They shall teach no more his brother, saying, Know the Lord: for they shall

all know Me, from the least of them unto the greatest of them, saith the Lord." Jer. 31:34. This condition is not achieved by men's own worthiness. It is a covenant that is established upon promises, made to sinners, and the Holy Ghost applies it to all whose sins are forgiven. Heb. 10:15–17. When we recognize that we are not our own, to do with what we please, but that our bodies are the temples of the Holy Ghost, and every member is to be yielded as an instrument ofrighteousness unto God, He will take complete possession, and we shall be "filled with the knowledge of His will in all wisdom and spiritual understanding."

Whatever appears desirable in the life of Christ, men are called to partake of. His invitation given in the temple court is still the same today. "If any man thirst, let him come unto Me and drink." He reserves nothing for Himself, but makes all who receive Him joint heirs with Himself. Let none delay to drink now. Jesus said, "Yet a little while am I with you, and I go unto Him that sent Me. Ye shall seek Me, and shall not find Me: and where I am, ye cannot come." "Seek ye the Lord while He may be found, call ye upon Him while He is near: let the wicked forsake his way, and the unrighteous man his thoughts." Isa. 55:6, 7. It is our thoughts that keep us from God. His thoughts are as much above ours as the heavens are above the earth. God's thoughts received will lift men to heaven, even to the throne of Christ. Rev. 3:21. Those who continue to think their own thoughts will seek Christ in vain, for where He is they cannot come. For those who receive His word, He prays, "Father, I will that they also, whom Thou hast given Me, be with Me where I am, that they may behold My glory, which Thou hast given Me." John 17:24. Knowing the Lord now, by actual experience, learning His way by letting Him reveal it in us, prepares the way to a more perfect knowledge, when we shall see Him as He is. "For now we see through the glass, darkly; but then face to face; now I know in part; but then shall I know even as also I am known." 1 Cor. 13:12.

—February 16, 1899

Chapter 10
The Test of Truth

John 8:12, 31–36

There is no uncertainty in the Gospel of Christ. The difficulties which men imagine they see in it are all in themselves, and these will vanish as soon as they accept it. This assurance which Jesus gave is true: "I am the light of the world; he that followeth Me shall not walk in darkness, but shall have the light of life." John 8:12. The light of life is the very essence, the perfection, of light; it is light which one has in himself even as he has life because it is his life.

Life, light, and love, are three things that agree in one. "He that saith he is in the light, and hateth his brother, is in darkness even until now. He that loveth his brother abideth in the light, and there is none occasion of stumbling in him. But he that hateth his brother is in darkness, and walketh in darkness, and knoweth not whither he goeth, because that darkness hath blinded his eyes." There is, however, no need for anybody to walk in darkness, "because the darkness is past, and the true light now shineth." 1 John 2:8–11. Whoever walks in darkness walks only in the darkness that is in himself. "Darkness shall cover the earth, and gross darkness the people; but the Lord shall arise upon thee, and His glory shall be seen upon thee." Isa. 60:2. If the darkness were primarily upon the earth, it would be deeper there than on the people; but inasmuch as the denser darkness covers the people, it is evidence that the seat of darkness is in the people themselves. "Because iniquity shall abound, the love of many shall wax cold." Matt. 24:12. When love waxes cold, the light goes out, and death comes.

"Love is of God," for God is love. He is love because He is life and light. "God is light, and in Him is no darkness at all." 1 John 1:5. Jesus Christ is "the brightness of His glory." Heb. 1:3. He is the true light that lighteth every one that comes into the world, because His light is His own life, and none live except by Him; the life is the light of men. John 1:4, 9. He is the Word, and so it is that the entrance of the Word of God gives light. But this light is the light of life and love, for His commandment is life everlasting (John 12:50), and "this is the love of God, that we keep His commandments." 1 John 5:3.

Note how the words of Jesus are introduced: "Then spake Jesus again unto them, saying, "I am the light of the world." When had He said this before?—At no time had He said it directly, that we have any record of, but He had said only the day before, "He that believeth on Me, as the Scripture hath said, out of his belly shall flow rivers of living water." John 7:38. Believing on Him is receiving Him (John 1:12); thus the living water that flows from the one who believes on Him, is from the indwelling Christ, who is the fountain of living waters. We see therefore that since life is light, the water of life is the source of the light of those who follow Christ. How often we speak of "sparkling water." That may most truly be said of the river of life, because it is "a flood of light."

The blood is the life. We are saved by the life of Christ, that is, we have redemption through His blood. Everything therefore that is life to us is but a manifestation of the blood of Christ. We must not think that the blood of Christ is merely that portion that issued from the wounds of His body on Calvary, and that it fell on the ground and was drunk up by it, so that all talk about being washed in the blood and drinking the blood is only figurative. Not by any means. His blood is incorruptible, and it is real. It is today the life of every man on earth. It comes to us in the food that we eat, in the water we drink, in the air we breathe, and in the light that warms and cheers us. We must get rid of our narrow and gross ideas of Christ's life. His life is the Spirit, since the indwelling Spirit is Christ come to dwell in the heart. God manifests Himself in an infinite variety of ways. We have in our own bodies proof of the fact that the blood of Christ—our life—exists in all things that support our life, for our blood is formed from the food we eat, the water we drink, the air we breathe, and the sunlight. If we would see and acknowledge Christ in all these blessings of life, we should be walking in the light as He is in the light, and the blood of Christ would cleanse us from all sin. Is not the Gospel indeed good news? It is the good news that to every man is salvation come in the life of Christ, which shines in the light, and which breathes in the air. Truly, he who is not saved has no cause of complaint against God.

"Then said Jesus to those Jews which believed on Him, If ye continue in My word, then are ye My disciples indeed; and ye shall know the truth, and the truth shall make you free." John 8:31, 32. Again we repeat that certainty accompanies the Gospel of Christ. Whoever wishes to do the will of God, shall know. By faith we understand. We are not to guess at truth, not to speculate about it, not to be "ever learning, and never able to come to the knowledge of the truth," but to know it absolutely. Is it too much for a man to say that he knows that he lives? Do you chide a man for saying, "I am alive?" That is knowledge that a man has not to learn; he has not to go outside of himself for it; he does not need to ask anybody's opinion about it. But Jesus Christ is "the way, and the truth, and the life;" the life is the truth; the true light that lights every man is the truth itself. So every man may and should be able to know the truth as absolutely as he knows that he lives. By what means can it be determined that a man is alive?—By seeing if there is motion. If the heart beats, if we can detect the faintest flutter in any artery, showing that the blood is moving, we know that the man is alive. So even a dying man will demonstrate to us that life is not yet extinct, by moving a finger or turning his eyes. How much more can that man in whom there is abundance of life be sure of the fact. He can move his arms freely; he can leap and shout; there is free action in every muscle. He knows that he lives, and if some croaking skeptic should chide him for his positiveness, saying, "You should not express yourself so confidently; you may say that you *think* you live, or you hope you are alive, but it is altogether too presumptuous for you to say that you *know* you are alive, at least until you have had a council of doctors," he would laugh in his face. This same joyous confidence may anybody have as to his absolute knowledge of the truth.

Just as we know that we live, by the working of life in us, so may we know the truth by what it does. It gives freedom. "Every one that committeth sin is the bondservant of sin. And the bondservant abideth not in the house forever; the Son abideth ever. If, therefore, the Son shall make you free, ye shall be free indeed." There is no bondage but sin, even as sin alone is death. But the truth is life, and the truth of life makes the conscious possessor of it free from sin. Truth is not a theory, a dogma, a creed, but it is life—*the life*. Whatever a man holds that does not make any difference in his life, is not truth; but everything that gives a man freedom from something that binds him, is truth.

The statement of truth is not the truth itself, any more than the recipe for making bread is food. A man might have a perfect knowledge of the proper food elements for the nourishment of the body, and might know how they should be combined, and might be able to tell just how every dish should be prepared and might starve to death while telling it. Even so a man may have a perfect theory of truth and yet not know the truth, because he has not yielded himself to its quickening influences; he may die while talking about life. A man knows only what he experiences, and experience is life. Only that man knows the truth, in whom the truth is the life.

There is no attempt in this to disparage statements of truth. It is well to have a perfect form; but the form of a man, without life, is nothing. A man may say, "I believe," and go on to recite a creed in which the keenest theologian or Bible student can detect no flaw, and still be densely ignorant of the truth. No creed or formula, however true it is, is *the truth*, for the truth is *the life*. For example, chemists tell us that the formula for sugar is $C_6H_{12}O_6$. That is, sugar is composed of six molecules of carbon, twelve of hydrogen, and six of oxygen. Now a person may know all that, and may repeat the formula a thousand times without once having a sweet taste in his mouth. That formula is not sugar; it simply stands to the eye of the chemist instead of the word; it is a description, but it is not the thing itself.

There is not a soul that has not been at some time conscious of being in bondage. "For the flesh lusteth against the Spirit, and the Spirit against the flesh; and these are contrary the one to the other; so that ye cannot do the things that ye would." Gal. 5:17. This is something real; it is no theory. When a man wishes to do something, and finds himself bound, or is compelled to do something that he does not wish to do, he is painfully conscious of the reality. Now if that which he holds as truth enables him to do the good that he would do, and to refrain from the evil that he would not do; yea, more than this, if it enables him to wish to do the good which before he shrank from, and to abhor the evil which he once loved, then to the extent that this is true, he has the truth. The truth makes free. "Where the Spirit of the Lord is, there is liberty" (2 Cor. 3:17), "because the Spirit is truth." 1 John 5:6.

Let nobody rest content that he has all the truth, because he knows something of this freedom. Many a near-sighted man has supposed that he could see as well as anybody, until he put on spectacles. It is possible for a person to become so accustomed to a cramped position as to feel quite comfortable in it. To move from it may cause him pain, but when he is fully aroused he is conscious of a buoyancy and freedom that he did not know before. The ignorant man may think that he knows everything; but when knowledge actually comes to him, he knows it, and knows that formerly he was ignorant. A man may be mistaken in his ideas of knowledge and freedom while he is ignorant and in bondage, but when light and freedom come there is no mistaking them. "Always more to follow" is true of God's gifts; so let every soul know that there is always greater measure of freedom and larger measure of life yet before him.

Jesus Christ is the truth. Notice how He uses the words "the Son" as synonymous with "the truth." He says: "If ye continue in My word, then are ye My disciples indeed; and ye shall know the truth, and the truth shall make you free. ... If the Son therefore shall make you free, ye shall be free indeed." So just as one may know the truth, so may we know Christ. It is possible to make His personal acquaintance, and know Him better than we know anybody else in the world. "We know that the Son of God is come, and hath given us an understanding, that we may know Him that is true, and we are in Him that is true, even in His Son Jesus Christ. This is the true God, and eternal life." 1 John 5:20. He who knows not this knows nothing; he who knows this truth has the key to "all the treasures of wisdom and knowledge."

—February 23, 1899

Chapter 11
How Not to Believe

A wonderful contrast is presented in the ninth chapter of John between the simplicity of faith and the bewildering windings of unbelief. A man who had been born blind had had his sight given to him by Jesus, and the short work that this man made of all the sophistries and arguments of the Pharisees, showed that Christ's miracle had given him clearness of mental as well as physical vision. The spirit which rested upon Jesus, making Him "of quick understanding in the fear of the Lord" (Isa. 11:3), was the same spirit by which He was anointed for the "recovering of sight to the blind" (Luke 4:18). Christ's work for man is not a partial one. All manner of blindness is the work of Satan, and "for this purpose the Son of God was manifested, that He might destroy the works of the devil."

As Jesus, with His disciples, passed the blind man, they asked Him, saying, "Master, who did sin, this man, or his parents, that he was born blind? Jesus answered, Neither hath this man sinned, nor his parents: but that the works of God should be made manifest in him. I must work the works of Him that sent Me, while it is day: the night cometh, when no man can work. As long as I am in the world, I am the light of the world."

We may learn from these words why any sickness or infirmity is allowed to come upon men. It all comes because of sin, but not in any spirit of vengeance or retaliation. The object is not to punish, but in order that the works of God should be made manifest in us. This appears clearly in the case of the blind man. The works of God were finished from the foundation of the world (Heb. 4:3, 4), and one of those works was to cause the light to shine out of darkness. What made the light shine in the beginning? We have the answer in John's record, "As long as I am in the world, I am the light of the world." But in being the light of the world, Jesus was working the works of Him that sent Him; therefore, we know that when God said, "Let there be light," the light shone because God Himself is light.

That same light is not only for the eyes but for the spiritual sight also. The same "God who commanded the light to shine out of darkness, hath shined in our hearts, to give the light of the knowledge of the glory of God in the face of Jesus Christ." 2 Cor. 4:6. And in both cases, the operation is performed in the same way. God Himself is light, therefore He shines. Whoever sees the sunlight sees the light which shone out of darkness, and so sees the shining of God. "The heavens declare the glory of God." But whoever recognizes the shining of God in the light opens his heart to the same shining, and it shines in his heart as spiritual light. But God is a Spirit, therefore is spiritually discerned; so that whoever worships Him in spirit and in truth, sees as much more in the shining as the spirit excels the flesh in the ability to discern God. While the natural eye can only see the brightness, the shining into the heart gives "the light of the knowledge of the glory of God in the face of Jesus Christ." Thus is realized the blessed truth that it is Jesus Christ who is the light of the world. "If we say that we have fellowship with Him, and walk in darkness, we lie, and do not the truth; but if we walk in the light, as He is in the light, we have fellowship with one another, and the blood of Jesus Christ His Son, cleanseth us from all sin." 1 John 1:6, 7.

All this was given to men when the light shone out of darkness in the beginning, for the works were finished from the foundation of the world, but because of unbelief men failed to enter into the rest which the completion of God's works secured to them; therefore it was necessary, over and over again, "that the works of God should be made manifest." Just as God commanded the light to shine out of darkness, by letting the shining of His own life appear, so in all His works He was simply revealing Himself. The work of creation was simply the fuller manifestation, to created intelligences, of His own existence. Therefore all that Christ had to do to work the works of God was to live the life of God.

All His wonderful works were simply the revelation of that life. So when He gave sight to the blind man, He simply showed what He was, the light of the world. Thus only can we work the works of Him who has sent us into the world, as He sent Jesus Christ. The Jews said to Jesus, "What shall we do, that we might work the works of God? Jesus answered and said unto them, This is the work of God, that ye believe on Him whom He hath sent." John 6:28, 29. To believe on is to receive. Let Jesus abide in you, and you, too, just as He did, will do the works of God. Be sure that He dwells in your heart by faith,—and you may be sure, for He stands at the door of every heart and knocks for admittance,—and the works of God will certainly appear. "As many as received Him, to them gave He power to become the sons of God." John 1:12.

In giving the light to the world God gives Himself, but men ignore the gift, so that it becomes necessary for Him to manifest it more emphatically. He does not withdraw the gift because His goodness is contemptuously despised, but seeks to impress men with the value of that which He bestows. Therefore men are permitted sometimes to experience the horrors of darkness, that they may be led to appreciate more highly the inestimable blessing of light. The man in this lesson was born without sight that he might one day see with joy the light which his countrymen would blind their eyes to. Had it not been for his many years of blindness, he, like them, might have despised the light of the world; but, as it was, the wonderful work of God was made manifest in him.

Notice how the stubborn unbelief of the Jews entrenches itself behind the unanswerable question, "*How* did Jesus make the blind man to see?" They could not deny the fact, although they sought to do so, but again and again, they brought up the same difficulty, which was no difficulty at all. "*How* was it done?" See verses 10, 15, 19, 26. It was the same with Nicodemus, "*How* can a man be born when he is old." No man can know how God works. If we were infinite, we would know how the world was created, and how the Son of God became a babe, and rose again from the dead, but not being infinite, we cannot tell how any of God's works are done. We cannot tell how the grass grows, and we cannot tell how God can dwell in human hearts, but we may know that He does it. We may be like the man in the lesson: "One thing I know, that whereas I was blind, now I see." We cannot know how God shines into our hearts the light of the knowledge of His glory in the face of Christ, but since He has so shined unto all, and only the minds of those that believe not are darkened (2 Cor. 4:3, 4), every one may know surely that He has so shined; and that whereas we were blind to that wonderful light, now we see.

The faith that God asks of men is reasonable, for it deals with facts. God does not ask us to exercise what some people understand by faith, a mysterious form of mental exercise which is supposed to be able to evolve something out of nothing. He just asks us to accept existing facts, to rest on the works which were finished from the foundation of the world. It is unbelief that is unreasonable. If some clever satirist had attempted to depict the follies of unbelief, he could not possibly have heaped more ridicule upon it than the Jews, who figure in the ninth chapter of John, heaped upon themselves forevermore when they sought to overthrow the simple fact that Christ had given sight to the blind. As a lesson in how not to believe, it stands unsurpassed. If any wish to escape the clearest evidences of truth, they may be recommended to this example, and to the arguments employed on this occasion.

Observe how thoroughly the ground was covered. First, the Pharisee asked how the miracle was done. When told of the means employed, they pronounced the miracle impossible because the Healer was out of harmony with their conceptions of God, and the proper observance of the Sabbath. Then when the man expressed his belief that Christ was a prophet, it suggested doubts of his veracity, and they refused to believe that he had been born blind. Having agreed to excommunicate whoever should confess that Jesus was the Messiah, they next questioned the man's parents, but these, although declining to commit themselves as to the work of Christ, were clear that their son had been blind and was now able to see. Assuming a deep piety, and recognizing at last that the miracle was beyond question, they again saw the man and endeavoured to inspire in him a holy horror of the sinner who had restored his sight. But sinner or no, he had a decent gratitude to his benefactor, and queried why they should so anxiously concern themselves unless they intended to become Christ's disciples. "Then they reviled him." The light that had shone into this man's life was Christ Himself, and this was made manifest, for this man spoke with the clearness and wisdom that Christ Himself displayed. Then the Pharisees used their last, crowning argument, and excommunicated the man. The light was revealing itself in him, but they hated the light, and banished it from them.

If any man chooses darkness rather than light and desires to know how to encourage and strengthen unbelief, let him be like the Jews. Refuse to acknowledge any fact, however indisputable, unless the means can be explained to your satisfaction. Believe nothing that you cannot understand. When others, in their simplicity, believe the Word of God and find in it healing and power, refuse to accept their testimony unless they can explain how it was done. If this does not shake their confidence, then revile them. It is probable that they will not be affected by this, and, if not, as far as your power extends, excommunicate them. There will always be plenty to side with you, indeed you may safely reckon on a majority of the disputers and the wise of this world, and when you finally discover yourself with the "unbelieving" (Rev. 21:8, 22:15), on the wrong side of the "wall great and high," which surrounds the city of God, you may find a last consolation in the reflection that the redeemed inside the city cannot explain *how* it is that they are there.

—March 2, 1899

Chapter 12

The Good Shepherd

John 10:1–16

In excommunicating the man whose sight Christ had restored, the Pharisees showed that the motive which ruled their actions was a jealous regard for their own dignity and honour, rather than a tender concern for the true welfare of the people who looked to them for spiritual guidance. Mankind are often referred to in the Scriptures as sheep, and in habits and disposition they show the fitness of the comparison. The Lord recognizes it Himself, and He desires to be to us what a faithful shepherd is to his flock. "He is our God; and we are the people of His pasture, and the sheep of His hand." Ps. 95:7. "The Lord is my Shepherd, I shall not want. He maketh me to lie down in green pastures: He leadeth me beside the still waters." Ps. 23:1, 2. "And ye My flock, the flock of My pasture are men, and I am your God, saith the Lord God." Ezek. 34:31.

The Shepherd Himself was now come to seek and to save that which was lost. Those to whom the care of the flock had been committed, had too often proved themselves thieves and robbers, and the sheep had been scattered. "My sheep wandered through all the mountains, and upon every high hill: yea, My flock was scattered upon all the face of the earth, and none did search or seek after them." "Woe be to the shepherds of Israel that do feed themselves! should not the shepherds feed the flocks? Ye eat the fat, and ye clothe you with the wool, ye kill them that are fed: but ye feed not the flock. The diseased have ye not strengthened, neither have ye healed that which was sick, neither have ye bound up that which was broken, neither have ye brought again that which was driven away, neither have ye sought that which was lost; but with force and with cruelty have ye ruled them. And they were scattered, because there is no shepherd: and they became meat to all the beasts of the field, when they were scattered." Ezek. 34. Because of this the Lord says, "Behold I, even I, will both search My sheep, and seek them out."

In the performance of this work the Good Shepherd was brought into conflict with the false shepherds. These desired to retain their control of the flock, not that they might do them good, but for the sake of the influence which their position procured for them. They were hirelings, only caring for the emoluments of their office, and ignoring its duties and responsibilities. Christ came to reveal to all the character of the true shepherd. Although every one, like sheep, had turned each to his own way, still all were sheep, and the Shepherd came not to condemn but save. Yet none could be saved unless they should turn from the evil of their way and live.

Jesus proclaims Himself to be the one door by which the sheep may find entrance to the fold. He is the way, the truth and the life. So He is the living way, and He is the living door. No one can enter into the fold who does not live the life of Christ. Whoever can say, like Paul, "I live, yet not I, but Christ liveth in Me," is in the way, and can go through the door. "He shall be saved, and shall go in and out, and find pasture."

But this is not the end. While we are always the flock of Christ, when we have His life in us, we are also to be shepherds to others, that they too may be led to enter through the door. "He that entereth in by the door is the shepherd of the sheep." This responsibility rests upon every soul. We cannot say like Cain, unless we share his spirit and his destiny, "Am I my brother's keeper?" and Christ has answered for every one the question of those that are willing to justify themselves, "Who is my neighbor?" We must either gather with Christ or scatter abroad. We are either true shepherds, or false ones.

There is only one way of becoming a true shepherd, and that is by receiving the life of Christ. This does not merely consist in agreeing verbally to what the Lord says. The life of Christ is as real as our physical life, for it is only by His life that we live at all. Our lives are just what we are in word, deed and thought. The life of Christ is just what He is, in every detail of His life. Whoever receives Christ's life will live as He does, in thought, word and deed. Whoever comes short of that life commits sin, which is coming short of the glory of God. Rom. 3:23. Whoever comes short of the glory of God, no matter how high his profession may be, is living a sinful life. But Jesus came to save His people from their sins; therefore, He came that we might, in our lives, be filled with all the fullness of God, and not come short of His glory. Our own thoughts and words and deeds are not to appear. "For if we have been planted together in the likeness of His death, we shall be also in the likeness of His resurrection." "Yield yourselves unto God, as those that are alive from the dead, and your members as instruments of righteousness unto God." Rom. 6. "If Christ be in you, the body is dead because of sin; but the Spirit is life because of righteousness." Rom. 8:10.

Jesus makes the issue a very plain one. The shepherd who lives to himself, or by himself, at all, is not one who may develop into a true shepherd. He never will. The command to men is not to train and discipline their thoughts, but to forsake them. Isa. 55:7. Let the wicked forsake his way. Christ is the living way, and no man comes into the fold except by that way. Christ did not come to combine Himself with men, but to save them from themselves. Light has no fellowship with darkness. Everywhere shepherds are feeding the flock with their own words. They themselves are not properly identified with Christ, but self is allowed to appear. Christ says of all such that they are thieves and robbers. Only the one who is emptied of self, and lets the mind of Christ guide him entirely can feed the flock with unselfish, Christ-like care.

Notice some of the characteristics of the true shepherd, and remember that these, and every other feature of Christ's life, must be reproduced in the under-shepherds, because the only way for them is the way of Christ's life.

The sheep hear His voice. The true shepherd will not speak of himself, but as the oracles of God. Jesus' life was just the Word made flesh, and His followers are to live by every word that proceedeth out of the mouth of God. In this way, the word will be the spring of all their actions, not of a few, but of all. The words of God are not merely articulate sounds, but being alive, they are things. Our food which grows by the creative power of the word, is the word made food, and in our lives, the word is to appear as a living thing, taking its shape from us, but having all the life and power in itself. We are to be the word made flesh, and through us the word will speak to the scattered and wandering sheep in words and deeds of tender love and helpfulness. The sheep will recognize the voice of the Shepherd, and will follow the loving call. Let the word of God dwell in us richly in all wisdom, so that there is nothing in our lives which is not the working of the word, and Christ, being lifted up, will draw all unto Him."

"He calleth His own sheep by name." Successful work does not consist in dealing with the multitudes, but with individuals. The work is not given to a favoured few. It is "to every man his work." Self-love and self-seeking prompt a desire for the most public place where all may see and admire. The true shepherd leaves the ninety and nine and goes after that which is lost until he find it. So will it be with all who have the true shepherd heart that all receive who enter the sheep-fold by the way of Christ's life. He "leadeth them out. And when he putteth forth his own sheep, he goeth before them, and the sheep follow him." The true shepherd does not delegate to others the difficult and unpleasant parts of the work. He goes before them. Christ is to men not merely a set of regulations, but a life. So far as men may be to others what Christ is to them, His followers are to be to those to whom they minister, not merely words of instruction but a living example. The true shepherd lives before his flock the truths which he proclaims. He is foremost in every good word and work. He does not preach and expect others to practice, but he preaches mainly by his practice.

The likeness between the Chief Shepherd and the under-shepherds is not to stop at any point. The Good Shepherd giveth His life for the sheep, and those who share His life will also give theirs. The Lord promises all who thus partake of His sufferings that they shall share His joy. Through them He will perfectly manifest Himself to the flock. "I am the good Shepherd, and I know Mine own, and Mine own know Me, even as the Father knoweth Me, and I know the Father." The closeness of the relation between Christ and the Father sets forth the intimate relation which Christ will establish between Himself and His flock. As they two are one, so all His people are to be one with Himself and each other. When this is true they will be successful as soul winners. The Lord will be able to reveal Himself through them as the true Shepherd, and to bring in by their means the sheep which are outside the fold, so that there shall be one fold and one shepherd.

—March 9, 1899

Chapter 13
Saved and Kept

The utter helplessness of men is often insisted upon in the Scriptures, but it is never intended to produce discouragement. The Saviour told His disciples that He sent them forth as sheep in the midst of wolves, but they were not to be alarmed over this, for the assurance is given, "My sheep hear My voice, and I know them, and they follow Me: and I give unto them eternal life; and they shall never perish, and no one shall snatch them out of My hand. My Father, which hath given them unto Me, is greater than all, and no one is able to snatch them out of the Father's hand. I and the Father are one." John 10:27–30. Not their own weakness but the strength of the Father and the Son is the measure of the security which the sheep enjoy.

What is it that causes men to be numbered among the sheep? It is the relation they sustain to the Shepherd. They may be like the sheep, naturally stupid, easily led into danger, and entirely unable to look after themselves in the absence of the shepherd, but if, with all these natural weaknesses, they trust implicitly to the guidance and protection of the True Shepherd; they will be delivered from the evils into which they would fall if left to themselves. "My sheep hear My voice ... and they follow Me." So long as they sustain this relation, the promise is theirs: "They shall never perish and no one shall snatch them out of My hand." That which precludes the possibility of the sheep being lost is the fact that they hear the voice of the Shepherd and follow Him. Thus they experience what Christ declares to be the portion of His flock: "I am the good Shepherd; and I know Mine own, and Mine own know Me, even as the Father knoweth Me, and I know the Father." Verses 14, 15. Unspeakably close and tender is the tie between the Saviour and those who follow Him. Nothing can be compared with it except the wondrous love that unites in one the Father and His only begotten Son.

A great many people who claim for themselves the promise that they shall never perish, show that they have no real appreciation of its meaning, and that they do not know it in the only way it can be known, by practical experience. Yet such generally claim for themselves that they have entered upon a plane of spiritual life, which is far above the average Christian experience. In many instances when the true Sabbath of the Lord is brought to their notice they refuse to listen to the voice which spoke from heaven the ten commandments, although they claim to be His sheep. If it be pointed out to them that disobedience to God's commands is sin (1 John 3:4), and that the wages of sin is death (Rom. 6:23), they reply that it will not be so with them, because they have been born again, and Christ has promised that they shall never perish. Thus they take the promises of Christ to strengthen themselves in continuing to transgress His commandment, after the sin has been brought to their knowledge.

Almost invariably the people who use these arguments hold also the view that a person who has once been saved can never be lost, and they base this idea on the words of Christ that no man shall pluck His sheep out of His hand. A young lady who believed thus said recently that it would take away all her peace of mind if she could not believe that whatever she did she would never be finally lost.

This shows a pitifully narrow view of God's character and great work of salvation. This is not of so precarious a nature that no one can rejoice in it unless he feels that God has somehow committed Himself, so that He cannot cast a person off even if, on account of subsequent developments, He should wish to. There is assurance enough in God's own love to render salvation secure to anyone who can possibly be saved. The theories we have referred to are an invention of Satan to keep people selfishly content not to know the depth of God's love, which does not need to be tied down to the task of saving a person, but, freely and gladly, does more for men than they can ask or think. As usual, when men thus pervert the Scriptures, the comfort which they think they get so much more certainly by their own interpretation turns out to be no comfort at all. No one can deny that both in the Scriptures, and in private life, men who have once served God, turn from Him and die impenitent. You ask a believer in the theory of "once in grace, always in grace," how he reconciles his views with these undoubted facts, and he will reply, "Oh, they were never really born again, or they could not have fallen away." "But while they were professing Christians, they themselves and all about them believed that they were born again. How can you be any more sure than they that you are not mistaken and that you also will not fall away? They were as positive as you are now that they were born again." The divine warning is given, "Let him that thinketh he standeth, take heed lest he fall." It is clear, therefore, that this certainty is no certainty at all, and can give no real comfort.

People who take such a position, in doing so give evidence that they are not born of the Spirit, for their very attitude springs from a carnal mind. This same spirit is manifested in many who want to be saved, but who find in the world and the flesh attractions which exceed the drawing power of Christ over their hearts. They wish that the Lord would take them by force and save them all at once, in such a way that they would not have power to yield to temptation in the future. They would give anything if this could be done for them. They would be willing to hand over their future to the Lord if He would deal with it by one operation. They do not like the process of being continually saved from sin, because often their own inclinations are uppermost, and it means a struggle to them to allow the Lord to save them from the sin they want to commit.

But there is perfect freedom with the Saviour. "Where the Sprit of the Lord is there is liberty." The Son makes men free; there is no slavery of any description where He reigns, for He will reign by love or not at all. The Lord never presumes on anything that has gone before. He does not say to Christians, "No, I cannot allow you to commit this sin. I have taken too much pains with you, and suffered too much to think of allowing you to do as you please now, unless you do as I please. You promised to follow Me, and I intend to hold you to your promise now, whether you like it or not." If a Christian should say, "When I promised to follow you, I did not know how attractive the world could be. I really prefer in this instance to go my own way," the Lord will not compel an unwilling obedience. In the Lord's service every soul is perfectly free to go on or turn back. Jesus has the satisfaction of knowing that every soul who follows Him, does so simply and solely because he prefers His company to anything else. There are no vows to bind them, after the love has waxed cold. The one tie that unites Christ to His people is love. In this freedom consists the joy of the relationship. The gladdest thought of the redeemed is that they are the chosen of Christ, and as He looks over the hosts of the redeemed, His own infinite love finds satisfaction in the thought that there is not one among them who would not freely sacrifice all for Him.

How much more encouraging is the promise that Christ actually makes to His sheep. The foregoing is not written to minimize in the least the confidence which the Christian may feel in his final salvation, but only to show how much more secure God's promises make it than men's ideas can. There is no lack of assurance for the future. Paul declares that neither death nor life, nor things present nor things to come shall be able to separate us from the love of God, which is in Christ Jesus. Rom. 8:38, 39. For all things are yours; whether Paul or Apollos, or Cephas, or the world, or life, or death, or things present, or things to come; all are yours; and ye are Christ's." 1 Cor. 3:22, 23. But the Scriptures also make known that the hope of these things is a living hope.

Therefore the life of them is now ours to enjoy, and whatever power the future will reveal in the things which God hath prepared for them that love Him, that power is for us now, if we lay hold of the hope. Thus among the things which go to make up the privileges of the Christian, we read of "the powers of the world to come." Heb. 6:5.

So we read concerning Christ's sheep, "I give unto them eternal life and they shall never perish." To perish is the very opposite of having eternal life. God gave His Son that believers should not *perish* but have *eternal life.* John 3:16. How does Christ give the eternal life? "The words that I speak unto you they are Spirit and they are life." John 6:63. "My sheep hear My voice." In speaking to us, Christ gives us eternal life, and those who thus receive eternal life shall never lose it, "they shall never perish." In this way we may know for certain whether we have eternal life, for we may know whether we receive His Word or not. And just as long as we want to retain eternal life, we may be sure that we are retaining it by continuing to hear His voice.

Men do not value the Word of God as they should, because they do not sufficiently appreciate how different it is to all human speech. Unlike the words of men, it is full of eternal life and power. This is why it is able to build us up and give us an inheritance among the sanctified. Acts 20:32. Those who receive it as it is, not a human word but the all-powerful Word of God, find that it works mightily in them. They, by receiving the Word, receive into themselves the power of God, so great that none can pluck them out of His hand. Only the reversal of the process which brought them into the Father's hand can take them out of that protection. Unbelief will hide the power of God from them, and leave them helpless, but self-doomed victims to Satan.

In the hand of God men are safe from all harm. That hand will lead them and hold them in safety and righteousness. It is so strong that it does not need to grip them in a vice-like clutch to preserve them from evil. Its clasp is an infinitely tender and loving one. "Yea, He loved the people; all His saints are in Thy hand: and they sat down at Thy feet; every one shall receive of Thy words." Deut. 33:3.

—March 16, 1899

Chapter 14
The Glory of God

John 11:32-45

Jesus was in a retired place beyond Jordan, whither He had gone to escape the continual persecutions of the Jewish rulers. There He taught the people in quiet, "and many believed on Him there." John 10:42. While He was there, one of His dearest friends fell ill, and his sisters sent word to Jesus, saying, "Lord, he whom Thou lovest is sick." John 11:3. "When Jesus heard that, He said, This sickness is not unto death, but for the glory of God, that the Son of God might be glorified thereby." Verse 4. Yet Lazarus died. What shall we say, therefore? What should we say if it were a present instead of a past occurrence? If we had received the assurance that our loved one's sickness was not unto death, but for the glory of God, and he was now lying cold and lifeless? Would we say that the word of the Lord had failed? That either the Lord had made a mistake, or else we had misunderstood His words? That is what we should be likely to say, but it is just what we ought not to say. "The word of the Lord shall stand forever." Although Lazarus had been dead for days, his sickness was not unto death, but for the glory of God. Can you believe the word of the Lord even when it is very "*apparent*" that it has failed? That is faith; and faith that will not be shaken by anything that appears, will bring victory out of defeat, and life from the dead.

At last the Master had come to the home where He had passed many pleasant hours in unrestrained, quiet, Christian fellowship. He was met with the words, "Lord, if Thou hadst been here, my brother had not died." Verse 21, also 32. This was the greeting of each sister. It almost seemed as if the Friend had been indifferent. He had tarried two whole days after hearing of the sickness of Lazarus, before making any movement toward going to see him. Oh, glorious indifference! It was the indifference of Omnipotence,—not indifferent to human suffering and human need, but indifferent to the threats of a foe whose utmost power could avail nothing. It was the immovable calm that comes from the consciousness of "all power." No one can by any means pluck a single soul out of the hand of the great Shepherd. The gates of the grave cannot prevail against one of those whom He bears upon His heart.

What need to be in a hurry? "He that believeth shall not make haste." Suppose the grave did close for a moment upon one whom it claimed as its prey: that proved nothing. When a general was informed in the heat of the battle that the day was lost, he coolly replied, "Very well, we'll take it again," and he did. Defeat was but a step to victory. So death did not disconcert the One who could say, "I am the Resurrection and the Life: he that believeth in Me, though he were dead, yet shall he live; and whosoever liveth and believeth in Me, shall never die." Verses 25, 26. What a marvelous confidence in the power of the Father, was manifested in the *seeming* indifference of Jesus! He claimed nothing for Himself; He acknowledged that He had no power in Himself; but He knew whom He had believed, and in quietness and in confidence was His strength. What a lesson of trust there is for us in this story of Jesus and Lazarus. "Trust ye in the Lord forever; for in the Lord Jehovah is everlasting strength."

"Jesus wept." So did Mary and Martha, and so did the Jews who had come to condole with them. They all wept. But whoever supposes that Jesus wept as the rest did, makes a great mistake. It is unfortunate that none of our English versions indicate any distinction here, for there is a marked difference. In the Greek two different words are used, and some translations are faithful to it. The word used concerning Mary and Martha and the others is properly rendered "weep," and may be used to indicate any loud lamentation and wailing; but Jesus simply "shed tears." The fountain of Divine love and compassion is always full to overflowing. Jesus must shed tears at the sight of human anguish, even when He knew that the power was in His hands to remove it, and He was just on the point of doing so. Here is an example to us, that we may "sorrow not, even as others which have no hope. For if we believe that Jesus died and rose again, even so them also which sleep in Jesus will God bring with Him." 1 Thess. 4:13, 14. He who sorrows only with Jesus, and only as He sorrows, has such joy as the world knows nothing of.

"Jesus therefore again groaning in Himself cometh to the grave. It was a cave, and a stone lay upon it. Jesus said, take ye away the stone. Martha, the sister of him that was dead, saith unto Him, Lord, by this time he stinketh; for he hath been dead four days. Jesus saith unto her, Saith I not unto thee, that, if thou wouldst believe, thou shouldest see the glory of God? Then they took away the stone from the place where the dead was laid. And Jesus lifted up His eyes, and said, Father, I thank Thee that Thou hast heard Me. And I knew that Thou hearest Me always; but because of the people which stand by I said it, that they may believe that Thou hast sent Me. And when He had thus spoken, He cried with a loud voice, Lazarus, come forth! And he that was dead came forth, bound hand and foot with grave clothes; and his face was bound about with a napkin. Jesus saith unto them, Loose him, and let him go." John 11:38–44.

"Thou shalt see the glory of God." Did any dazzling light shine upon the company there assembled? There is no evidence of any such thing. Everything was quiet, and no light appeared to any, except the ordinary daylight; yet all present saw the glory of God. How?—In the power that was displayed in the resurrection of Lazarus. When Jesus turned the water into wine, at the marriage in Cana, "He manifested forth His glory." John 2:11. God's glory is His power, and that is His righteousness. "God is light" (1 John 1:5), so that His glory is His own Personality—His character—and since His glory is His power, we see that He is glorious and powerful because He is righteous.

That the power and the glory of God are the same, may be learned by comparing Rom. 6:4 and Eph. 1:17–20. In the former we read that "Christ was raised up from the dead by the glory of the Father," and in the second we read that the resurrection of Christ from the dead, and His elevation to the right hand of God in the heavenly places, was the result of the working of the "mighty power" of God. This power was "wrought in Christ," and, moreover, the Spirit of God earnestly desires that we may know the "exceeding greatness" of this power, which is "to usward who believe." Whatever the Spirit desires for us, we shall have if we consent to be led by the Spirit. Let us think what this means to us.

The glory of God is the power of the resurrection, and this power it is possible, nay, absolutely essential, for us to know. Phil. 3:10. We are exhorted thus, "Glorify God in your body." 1 Cor. 6:20. This can mean nothing less than that the power of Christ's resurrection is to be manifested in the bodies of Christians. But this is the power by which Lazarus was raised from the dead,—the power by which Christ was raised from the grave. And this means a power—the life of Christ—in men that will lift them above the power of death. "Always bearing about in the body the dying of the Lord Jesus, that the life also of Jesus might be made manifest in our mortal flesh." 2 Cor. 4:11.

The same thing is set forth in Rom. 8:10, 11. "If Christ be in you, the body is dead because of sin; but the Spirit is life because of righteousness. But if the Spirit of Him that raised up Jesus from the dead dwell in you, He that raised up Christ from the dead shall also quicken [make alive] your mortal bodies by His Spirit that dwelleth in you." The Spirit is life; therefore the Spirit cannot dwell in a man in fullness without imparting life to that man. The life of the Spirit makes the man live in spite of mortality. That this imparting of life is now, in the present world, and not something to be expected in some future state, is shown by the verse following: "Therefore, brethren, we are debtors, not to the flesh, to live after the flesh. For if ye live after the flesh, ye shall die; but if ye, through the Spirit, do mortify the deeds of the body, ye shall live." Having received the Spirit, we are debtors to live according to the Spirit, and not according to the flesh. That is to say, the Spirit gives us all His fullness, so that we owe everything to Him; but in that condition the flesh gives us nothing of its corruption, so that we owe nothing to it. But when the flesh gives us nothing of its corruption, then we are delivered from the bondage of corruption into the glory of the liberty of the sons of God.

The same truth is taught in Isa. 40:3–5: "The voice of Him that crieth in the wilderness, Prepare ye the way of the Lord, make straight in the desert a highway for our God. Every valley shall be exalted, and every mountain and hill shall be made low; and the crooked shall be made straight, and the rough places plain; and the glory of the Lord shall be revealed, and all flesh shall see it together; for the mouth of the Lord hath spoken it." Where is the way of the Lord to be prepared?—In men. The way of the Lord is prepared by preparing the people for the Lord. "And thou, child, shalt be called the prophet of the Highest; for thou shalt go before the face of the Lord to prepare His ways; to give knowledge of salvation unto His people in the remission of their sins." Luke 1:76, 77. The Lord's way is in the hearts and lives of His people. When that way is prepared, then the glory of the Lord must and will be revealed in His people; and the glory of the Lord is His life. It is by believing that we receive the Lord, and become sons of God; and thus it is that to us, as well as to the sisters of Lazarus, the words come, "If thou wilt believe, thou shalt see the salvation of God." What glorious things God has prepared for them that love Him!

"Loose him, and let him go." Christ came to set the captives at liberty. "I the Lord have called Thee in righteousness, and will hold Thine hand, and will keep Thee, and give Thee for a covenant of the people, for a light of the Gentiles; to open the blind eyes, to bring out the prisoners from the prison, and them that sit in darkness out of the prison house." Isa. 42:6, 7. But the word of reconciliation is committed to us; it is put into all who are reconciled. To men is entrusted the work which Jesus of Nazareth began. "Thus saith the Lord, In an acceptable time have I heard thee, and in a day of salvation have I helped thee; and I will preserve thee and give thee for a covenant of the people, to establish the earth, to cause to inherit the desolate heritages; that thou mayest say to the prisoners, Go forth; to them that are in darkness, Show yourselves." Isa. 49:8, 9. A comparison of this text with 2 Cor. 6:1, 2, will show that believers in Christ are the ones addressed. Not only are Christ's people to have the unconquerable life of Christ manifested in their own mortal flesh, but they are to minister it to others.

—March 23, 1899

Chapter 15
The Anointing at Bethany

John 12:1-11

"Jesus therefore six days before the passover came to Bethany, where Lazarus was, whom Jesus raised from the dead. So they made Him a supper there; and Martha served; but Lazarus was one of them that sat at meat with Him. Mary therefore took a pound of ointment of spikenard, very precious, and anointed the feet of Jesus, and wiped His feet with her hair; and the house was filled with the odour of the ointment. But Judas Iscariot, one of His disciples, which should betray Him, saith, Why was not this ointment sold for three hundred pence, and given to the poor? Now this he said, not because he cared for the poor, but because he was a thief; and having the bag took away what was put therein. Jesus therefore said, Suffer her to keep it against the day of My burying. For the poor ye have always with you; but Me ye have not always.

"The common people therefore of the Jews learned that He was there; and they came, not for Jesus' sake only, but that they might see Lazarus also, whom He had raised from the dead. But the chief priests took counsel that they might put Lazarus also to death; because that by reason of him many of the Jews went away, and believed on Him."

Six days before the passover means six days before the cross of Calvary. None of those who sat at the table with Jesus knew this; but Jesus knew it very well. Indeed, Jesus was always walking beneath the cross, for He knew from the beginning of His ministry what its end would be; and He knew just when the betrayal and crucifixion would take place, for He Himself had told His disciples about it as they were on their way to Jerusalem. Yet He was calm as at any other time. There was nothing in His looks or actions to mar the peace or joyousness of the feast.

What a lesson this contains for us. Jesus lived every day just as perfectly as He possibly could live on His last day; and therefore there was no need for Him to make some great change at the last. Most people would consider it an exhibition of recklessness or bravado, or else gross insensibility on the part of a man who should attend a feast six days from the time when he knew he was

The Anointing at Bethany

to suffer death; but we know that it was not so with Jesus. Why should He refuse to act in the last week of His earthy life just the same as He had always acted? Why spend time in mournful "preparations for death?" That always implies that one is conscious of a misspent life. No preparation is needed for death; all one has to do is to be prepared to live, and really live, and then if death does come, he will be ready for it, no matter how or when it comes.

If we put ourselves in the place of those disciples, we shall not wonder at their indignation over the seeming waste of the costly ointment. A reference to the record in the twenty-sixth chapter of Matthew shows that the other disciples were indignant, as well as Judas. How often have we expressed what we thought was "righteous indignation" over some supposed extravagance, or when something was done for which we could see no reason. We are very apt to make hasty judgments. May we not from this learn a lesson? We can see that it was wrong in this case; but it is not in itself so apparent as in many instances that come under our immediate notice. If the disciples had known all the circumstances, as we know them now, and as they did afterwards, none of them, save Judas, would have murmured.

The eleven disciples were sincere in their care for the poor, while Judas was a hypocritical thief: yet their zeal was altogether out of place. Indeed, they made themselves sharers in the sin of Judas, because he was the leader in the condemnation of Mary's act, since in this place he alone is mentioned as having complained. If they had known what spirit actuated him, they would not have thought of joining him in his outcry. Here again we may learn to be on our guard against sympathizing too readily with a man's grievance, and too readily joining in with somebody else's denunciation of what plainly seems to be a mistaken course. If we are not careful, we may be strengthening some traitor in his wicked designs, instead of helping the cause of suffering humanity.

When the disciples saw the whole box of ointment used upon Jesus, they said, "To what purpose is this waste?" Matt. 26:8. Think of spending the value of a whole year's labour in one gift, and that something that could be used only once! Three hundred pence meant three hundred days' labour. See Matt. 20:1, 2. But it was given freely, and Jesus did not reprove the giver, but on the contrary commended her. Nothing is wasted that is given to the Lord from a sincere heart. In the ancient days God's people used to burn up entire beasts upon the altar, and offer much costly incense, and God accepted it, yea, found delight in it. But God's pleasure in such service was dependent on the condition of the worshipper's heart. When the heart was filled with evil, incense was an abomination, and a multitude of whole burnt offerings was to no purpose. Isa. 1:10–13. But when the heart was purified by faith, and the sacrifice was one of joy for righteousness bestowed, then God was pleased, for "the sacrifices of God are a broken spirit." Ps. 51:17–19.

There is only one sacrifice that has ever been made, or that can ever be made, and that is the sacrifice of Christ. No man ever yet "made a sacrifice" for God. Many have "offered sacrifices," and sacrifices that have been acceptable, too, but they were sacrifices that God Himself provided. In the one sacrifice God has given us everything, and of His fullness, which we have all received, we are expected to make returns which serve, not to enrich Him, but to show our appreciation of and trust in His gift. The secret of every acceptable sacrifice is trust in God. "By faith Abel offered unto God a more acceptable sacrifice than Cain." Heb. 11:4. That which the one sacrificing really says,—that which his offering means,—is that which gives everything back to the Lord, and still be sustained. With Christ we receive all things from God. God has abundance of everything, and He gives lavishly. He not only sends rain on the unjust as well as on the just, but He causes it to rain on the wilderness, wherein there is no man. Job 38:26. Is it wasted? Oh, no; it will not return unto Him void. None of God's gifts are wasted, and nothing is wasted that is given to Him. Only by giving ourselves and all that we have to the Lord, can we be preserved. He that will save his life shall lose it, and he that will lose his life for Christ's sake shall save it unto life eternal.

What an example we have in this lesson of the blindness and wickedness of unbelief. Lazarus had been raised from the dead, and consequently much interest centered in him. The miracle had caused many to believe on Jesus. People flocked to see the man who had been dead four days, and buried, and who was now alive, and many of them went away believing. Now what did the unbelieving chief priests do? They were determined not to believe and not to allow anybody else to believe if they could help it; so they resolved to put Lazarus to death, so that this witness to the power of Christ might be removed. Yet they *thought* that they were working for the good of the people. Strange that they could not see that when they found it necessary to commit murder in order to sustain their position, that position must be wrong; for truth can never be sustained by violence and crime. "The wrath of man worketh not the righteousness of God." That shows the wickedness to which unbelief drives men. As to the blindness of it, think of their planning to kill a man that had been raised from the dead by and for the glory of God, in order to silence his living testimony as to the power of Christ to give life! How could they expect to kill him? They would be fighting directly against God. Even if the priests had been permitted to kill Lazarus, the result would necessarily have been his resurrection again under more striking circumstances than before. God makes even the wrath of man to praise Him, so that nobody can do anything against the truth, but for the truth. Who would not wish to be in harmony with a power that is so sure to succeed that even opposition helps it along?

—March 30, 1899

Chapter 16
Jesus Teaching Humility

John 13:1–17

The scripture that forms the lesson for this week is so rich, and so comprehensive in the instruction that it gives, that we quote it entire, from the Revised Version. The mere reading of the text cannot fail to benefit the reader. Give it careful and prayerful attention.

The Example

"Now before the feast of the passover, Jesus knowing that His hour was come that He should depart out of this world unto the Father, having loved His own which were in the world, He loved them unto the end. And during supper, the devil having already put it into the heart of Judas Iscariot, Simon's son, to betray Him, Jesus knowing that the Father had given all things into His hands, and that He came forth from God, and goeth unto God, riseth from supper, and layeth aside His garments; and He took a towel, and girded Himself. Then He poureth water into a basin, and began to wash the disciples' feet, and to wipe them with the towel wherewith He was girded. So He cometh to Simon Peter. He saith unto Him, Lord, dost Thou wash my feet? Jesus answered and said unto him, What I do thou knowest not now; but thou shalt understand hereafter. Peter saith unto Him, Thou shalt never wash my feet. Jesus answered him, If I wash thee not, thou hast no part with Me. Simon Peter saith unto Him, Lord, not my feet only, but also my hands and my head. Jesus saith to him, He that is bathed needeth not save to wash his feet, but is clean every whit; and ye are clean, but not all. For He knew him that should betray Him; therefore He said, Ye are not all clean.

"So when He had washed their feet, and taken His garments, and sat down again, He said unto them, Know ye what I have done to you? Ye call Me Master, and Lord; and ye say well; for so I am. If I then, the Lord and the Master, have washed your feet, ye also ought to wash one another's feet. For I have given you an example, that ye also should do as I have done to you.

Verily, verily, I say unto you, A servant is not greater than his lord, neither one that is sent greater than he that sent him. If ye know these things, blessed are ye if ye do them." John 13:1–17.

There we have the story; let us consider some of the wealth of instruction it contains for us. We cannot exhaust it. The most that can be done in this article will be merely to suggest some things for thought.

Not an Ordinary Occurrence

In the first place let it be noted that this was no common occurrence. Some people have imagined that this act of feet-washing was a thing rendered necessary by the fact that people wore low sandals, so that the feet became readily soiled and needed frequent washing, and that it was a common act of courtesy for a host to perform such a service for his guests. This is wholly imaginary. Suppose it were true, what kind of host would he be, who should neglect a thing that ought to be done when the guests first entered the house, if at all, until after they had sat down to supper? What would you think if you were invited to a feast, and in the midst of it were invited by your host to take a bath? No; the claim that the washing of feet was a common act of courtesy only sets Jesus forth as neglectful; and that fact alone disproves it.

It was indeed common for hosts to provide water for the feet of their guests, but not to wash their feet. Each one did that for himself. The host would no more think of washing the feet of his friends than we would think of washing the hands and faces of our friends when they arrive after a journey. We provide water for them, and leave them to make their own toilet. Even so it was in ancient times. Abraham was a pattern of hospitality, but he did not wash the feet of the three men whom he so courteously received. He ran to meet them, and bowing down to the ground, invited them to come in, saying, "Let a little water, I pray you, be fetched, and wash your feet, and rest yourselves under the tree; and I will fetch a morsel of bread, and comfort ye your hearts." Gen. 18:4, 5. Here we see very clearly that the guests were expected to wash their own feet. Hence it aroused the utmost astonishment on the part of the disciples, when they saw Jesus begin to wash their feet. They had never before seen or heard anything like that.

Christ as Servant

Who was it that did what even a common servant was not expected to do? It was Jesus, the Son of God. Was it because He lost sight of the dignity of His position, that He did it? Not at all; He did it in full consciousness that He came from God and was going to God. He knew that He was their Lord and Master, and nothing that He did was inconsistent with that fact. He did not lower Himself. Not one of His disciples had any the less respect for Him because of what He did. His was the true dignity that does not have to be hedged about in order to be preserved, but which preserves itself, and dignifies whatever it undertakes.

This was a lesson of service. Jesus said: "Ye know that the princes of the Gentiles exercise dominion over them, and they that are great exercise authority upon them. But it shall not be so among you: but whosoever will be great among you, let him be your minister; and whosoever will be chief among you, let him be your servant; even as the Son of man came not to be ministered unto, but to minister, and to give His life a ransom for many." Matt. 20:25–28. On this very occasion He said: "Whether is greater, he that sitteth at meat, or he that serveth? but I am among you as He that serveth." Luke 22:27. Jesus was greatest of all, because He did the humblest service.

"Let this mind be in you, which was also in Christ Jesus; who, being in the form of God, thought it not robbery to be equal with God; but made Himself of no reputation, and took upon Him the form of a servant, and was made in the likeness of men." Phil. 2:5–7. Notice that it was the *form*, not the character, of a servant, that Jesus took on Himself. Why did He not, in coming to earth, take the character of a servant?—Because He already had that. He came to earth to let the world see and know just what He was, but He had to come in a form that they could appreciate. Men's ideas were so perverted that if Jesus had come to earth in royal state and heavenly glory, they could never have associated Him with service, and so could not have learned the lessons of service that they ought. So He changed His *form*, and let His life show who He was. Those who recognize Him as Lord, and acknowledge Him as such, even while He bears the *form* of a servant, will one day have the privilege of seeing Him serve, and of being served by Him, when He is arrayed as King of kings, and Lord of lords; for He says to us: "Blessed are those servants, whom the Lord when He cometh shall find watching; verily I say unto you, that He shall gird Himself and make them sit down to meat, and will come forth and serve them." Luke 12:37.

Lowliness of the Most High

What an honour to be served by the King of glory! Yet just that honour we are all receiving every day; for the God of the universe has set and keeps all nature in operation to serve us. Day and night He waits to attend to every want. Every moment He watches, to see that we lack nothing. He gives to us life, and breath, and all things, and does service for us that no earthly servant could be hired to do, even if he had the power. Remember that Jesus was the revelation of God to men. Whoever saw Him saw the Father. John 14:9. Therefore the act of Jesus, in washing the feet of His disciples was designed to show us that the Most High God is the servant of all. Jesus Christ was "God manifest in the flesh." When Jesus said, "Learn of Me, for I am meek and lowly in heart," He was declaring the character of God. One does not ordinarily expect meekness and humility in kings' courts or in kings themselves; but the King of kings is meek and lowly in heart. Although He is "the high and lofty One," who dwells in "the high and holy place," He dwells also with him that is of a contrite and humble spirit. Isa. 57:15. His meekness constitutes His greatness, and it is only His gentleness that makes us great. Ps. 18:35.

We call Him Lord and Master; do we mean it? Is He our Lord? If so, then we are, and acknowledge ourselves to be, servants. "As He is, so are we in this world." He is Lord of servants, for He is Lord simply because He is servant. He is not to us the Lord unless we, like Him, are servants. He is Lord, not to *domineer* over His followers, but to *lead* them. The very name "disciples" or "followers," indicates that He is leader. And this shows absolute unity of purpose and character between them. They are as He is. He is different from them in degree only, not in kind. He is Lord, not because He rules while they serve, but because He does more service than they do. When we learn this, we shall know what our duty is in any position of authority in which we may be placed in the body of Christ.

The Dignity of Labour

The example of Christ in washing the feet of His disciples teaches us a lesson concerning the dignity of labour, and shows us that there is no such thing as "menial" labour. Any man who is ashamed of honest work, is not a follower of Christ, for the greater portion of His earthly life was spent as a carpenter. Anybody who looks with even the slightest degree of contempt upon one who is employed in the very lowest service, or who feels himself in any degree superior to a servant who is doing legitimate work in the very lowest position, is putting himself above Christ, and despising Christ. So long as the world stands there must be some who are what the world calls servants. There must necessarily be division of labour. No one person can do everything. Some are adapted to one thing, and others to another. But that which everybody ought to be taught is that all classes of honest and necessary work stand on an exact level. All who meet the end of their existence in this world, are servants. Read Col. 3:22–24; and 4:1: "Servants, obey in all things your masters according to the flesh; not with eye-service, as menpleasers; but in singleness of heart, fearing God; and whatsoever ye do; do it heartily, as to the Lord, and not unto men; knowing that of the Lord ye shall receive the reward of inheritance; for ye serve the Lord Christ." "Masters, give unto your servants that which is just and equal; knowing that ye also have a Master in heaven." Thus we see that all,—rich and poor, high and low,—are servants of the one Master. The fact that many refuse to recognize the relation does not nullify the truth. We see that for one to despise another who is called a servant, or who wears the garb of a servant, is to deny that he himself is a servant, and to despise his Master, who is, in both form and fact, a servant. It is not what one works at, but the spirit in which he works, that determines the grade of his service. Sweeping floors and blacking boots is just an honourable service as is preaching sermons or writing books. To guide a team of horses is in itself as dignified a calling as to guide a State; and the man who guides his team well, and as a worker for Christ, is more honourable than the one who guides the State without any thought of his responsibility to God. Learn from Christ that work is God's gift to man, and, when rightly done, allies man with God.

A Lesson of Love

Look again at the upper room where Jesus washed the feet of His disciples. Judas was among them, although the devil had already put it into his heart to betray his Lord, and the bargain had already been made with the chief priests. Jesus well knew what was in the heart of Judas, but the fellow-disciples of Judas did not. Jesus had all the time known the covetousness that was in the heart of Judas, and He knew that this covetousness would make him His betrayer. He knew the anger that filled the heart of Judas at his failure to secure the value of the ointment that had been poured out upon the Master. He saw Judas as he went to the chief priests and made the bargain which really meant murder. Nevertheless the Lord proceeded to wash the feet of Judas just the same as He did the others. No shade of difference was noticed in His treatment of them. Not by work, look, or gesture did Jesus give any intimation that He knew that Judas was not as loyal as the rest of the twelve. His intercourse with Judas, the traitor, was marked by the same tenderness as with John, the beloved disciple. Let those who are wont to consider feet-washing as an act of courtesy look at this phase of it for an example in courtesy such as the world has never seen.

But this was not an act of mere courtesy. It was the courtesy that naturally springs from perfect love. There was nothing "put on" with Jesus. He was just what He seemed to be. He did not force Himself to any line of action. In the world, the height of "good breeding" is manifested in the man who can maintain a calm exterior while boiling with indignation and rage within; but Jesus had that perfection of good breeding that the world never can know. It was the breeding that marks the oldest of "old families"—the family of God. He acted calmly, because was calm within. He made no difference in His treatment of the disciples, because He felt none. His was the character of God, who "maketh His sun to rise on the evil and on the good, and sendeth rain on the just and on the unjust." Matt. 5:45. "He is kind unto the unthankful and to the evil." Luke 6:35. Jesus treated Judas kindly, because He felt kindly toward him. In His heart there was not a trace of bitterness, no rising of anger, revenge, or what men delight in calling "righteous indignation." Yet Jesus "was in all points tempted like as we are." Heb. 4:15. He had our nature, so that injustice would tend to arouse Him as much as us. The perfect love which He manifested to all is a proof of the power of the Divine nature to swallow up the human. God gave Him "power over all flesh," so that the same unselfish love may be manifested in us.

The love that Jesus manifested in washing the feet of Judas was the same as that which prompted the prayer for those who crucified Him, "Father, forgive them, they know not what they do." He who washed the feet of Judas would just as readily have washed the feet of Pilate or the chief priests. And not only would He have washed the feet of these men, if occasion had called for it, but He would have performed any other service for them; for the feet-washing stood as the representative of all kinds of service for others. No man ever did a baser deed than Judas did; and the fact that Jesus did for him the most humble service, knowing that he was at the time under the direct influence of the devil, and planning the most heartless perfidy against his chief Benefactor, is evidence to us that Christ would gladly and lovingly serve His worst enemies. This is a strong ground of consolation to us, making it possible to come to Him with confidence, in spite of our sins against Him; but it is more than that; it is a lesson to us as to how we should treat those who might be considered our enemies.

An Example

There are very few of the professed followers of Christ who follow Him in the act of feet-washing, yet the commandment to do so is as explicit as any commandment found in the Bible. Listen: "If I then, your Lord and Master, have washed your feet, *ye also ought* to wash one another's feet. For *I have given you an example, that ye should do as I have done to you.*" Ye *ought* to wash one another's feet. That is, it is a duty; ye owe it to one another to do this. Suppose one could find in the Bible similar language concerning Sunday; how it would be seized upon. What would not the advocates of Sunday observance give for one such statement about that day. And if there were one such statement it would be decisive. When Jesus says that we ought to do anything, that should settle the matter with all His disciples; we ought to do it without any questioning. Things that we may not understand will be made clear to us in the performance. In keeping the commandments of the Lord there is great reward. Ps. 19:11. "If ye know these things, happy are ye if ye do them."

If ye know what things?—If he know that "the servant is not greater than his Lord; neither is he that is sent greater than He that sent him." If one knows that (and it is so simple that everybody ought to know it), it will be his greatest pleasure, and will consider an honour, to be permitted to do as His Lord does. Some have said that they "thought too much of themselves" to engage in any such act as the washing of feet. That is a sad condition to be in. That is to think more highly of self than one ought to think. It is to think ourselves greater than the One who sent us. No one can find any excuse for not following the example of Jesus, that will not be a condemnation of the Lord of glory.

But although the words of Jesus leave us no escape from a literal following of His example, the mere literal act of feet-washing is not a following of that example. We cannot do as He did, except in the same Spirit. If we have not the mind that was in Christ, we cannot do the works that He did. He who washes the feet of a brother, and at the same time cherishes the faintest shadow of ill will towards him, or has the slightest unbrotherly feeling, is not following the example of Christ. More than this, if there is in his heart any feeling of bitterness toward any soul on earth, he is not following the example of Christ, no matter how often he washes the feet of the brethren. If there is a lurking grudge in his heart, if he feels hurt and grieved because somebody has mistreated him, then he is not following the example of the Master; for Christ had no such feelings, and it is the condition of the heart that determines the value of any action. It is self-evident that no one can do as Christ did unless he is just as Christ was. Therefore it must be very plain to all that this ordinance of feet washing is calculated to bring all believers into absolutely perfect unity and harmony with Christ; and this would mean absolute harmony with one another, and perfect love for all men, even such love as led Jesus to give His life for His enemies. What a marvelous ordinance this is, that Christ has left in the church, to bring the members frequently to face the question whether they are imbued with His Spirit, and walking in His steps, or whether unconsciously they have been slipping away from Him!

One thing more should be noted: Jesus was anointed with the Holy Ghost and with power, and He "went about doing good, and healing all that were oppressed of the devil." Acts 10:38. He who follows Christ's example must likewise go about doing good, and ministering healing for all the ills that the devil brings upon men. He must be ready to give to any person any kind of help that is needed. He must be ready to give Christian help to all who need help, be they brethren in the faith or those who despise and hate the faith. "As we have therefore opportunity, let us do good unto all men, especially unto them who are of the household of faith." Gal. 6:10. The ordinance of feet-washing, which Christ Himself established in the church, is our profession of faith and practice—a mutual declaration that we have given ourselves to Christ, to do as He did,—a declaration that what we are doing for one another we are ready to do for anybody. If it does not mean this, it is but an empty form. But the Lord has no mere ceremonies in the church. The church is His body, and so must be filled with His life. What a blessed gift is this which He has provided for all His followers, that they may know that they are one with Him. Here we may know, as the visitor to old Jerusalem cannot, that we are walking in the footsteps of Christ, and that He is with us as we walk.

—April 16, 1899

Chapter 17
Words of Comfort

John 14:1–14

"I Will Come Again."

"Let not your heart be troubled; ye believe in God, believe also in Me. In My Father's house are many mansions; if it were not so, I would have told you. I go to prepare a place for you. And if I go and prepare a place for you, I will come again, and receive you unto Myself; that where I am, there ye may be also."

Jesus was personally present with His disciples when he spoke these words. He had been with them in bodily form for several years, and they had looked upon Him and handled Him, and had walked and talked with Him in loving companionship. His presence was as real as their own, and they delighted in it. But now He had told them plainly that He was going away, and that they could not follow Him. This had filled their hearts with sorrow; for they had yielded to the powerful attraction of Jesus, and since He had first said to them "Follow Me," to be with Him had been their joy. Now they felt as children do when the loved and loving mother is taken from them. They were in great heaviness of heart, and therefore Jesus spoke the comforting words that we have just read.

"The glorious appearing of our great God and Saviour Jesus Christ," is the "blessed hope" of all His true disciples. Titus 2:13. It is the comfort for all who mourn loved ones who have fallen in death. The words of the Apostle, direct from the Lord Himself, are: "I would not have you to be ignorant, brethren, concerning them which are asleep, that ye sorrow not, even as others which have no hope. For if we believe that Jesus died and rose again, even so them also which sleep in Jesus will God bring with Him. For this we say unto you by the word of the Lord, that we which are alive and remain unto the coming of the Lord shall not prevent [go before] them which are asleep. For the Lord Himself shall descend from heaven with a shout, with the voice of the Archangel, and with the trump of God; and the dead in Christ shall rise first; then we which are alive and remain shall be caught up together with them in the clouds, to meet the Lord in the air; and so shall we ever be with the Lord. Wherefore *comfort one another with these words.*" 1 Thess. 4:13–18.

One more text will be sufficient for the promise of His coming. Forty days after His resurrection, Jesus led His disciples out of Jerusalem "as far as to Bethany," telling them of the power by which they were to be witnesses to Him. "And when He had spoken these things, while they beheld, He was taken up, and a cloud received Him out of their sight. And while they looked steadfastly toward heaven as He went up, behold two men stood by them in white apparel; which also said, Ye men of Galilee, why stand ye gazing up into heaven? This same Jesus, which is taken up from you into heaven shall so come in like manner as ye have seen Him go into heaven." Acts 1:9, 10.

Looking at these statements, we see clearly that Jesus will come again, and that His coming will be as literal as was His first advent. "This same Jesus" is to return again. It is to be no secret coming, no snatching away of His people by stealth. No; the "voice of the Archangel and the trump of God" will make known the second coming of Christ, and every eye must see Him, whether it wishes to or not (Rev. 1:7), "for as the lightning cometh out of the east and shineth even unto the west; so shall also the coming of the Son of man be." Matt. 24:27.

Object of Christ's Coming

This is the all-important thing. Why will He come? What necessity is there for it? That His coming is necessary, is evident, since the Lord does nothing in vain. He will not come in all the pomp and splendour of heaven, with all His angels, and with earth-shaking peals of the trumpet, for nothing. The object is plainly stated in our text." I go to prepare a place for you. And if I go and prepare a place for you, I will come again, and receive you unto Myself; that where I am, there ye may be also." Take this in connection with the statement to the disciples, recorded in the preceding chapter (verse 36), "Whither I go, thou canst not follow [or, go with] Me now: but thou shalt follow Me afterwards," and we see that no words could make it plainer that only by the second coming of Christ in glory can His disciples be with Him again. It is not only those who chance to be living when He shall come, that He takes to Himself, but the eleven to whom He was talking. They can never be with their Master again, except by His coming again to receive them. Until He comes, they are away from Him.

Here is where the comfort comes in. When it is known that none can be with Christ except by His second coming, then everybody who loves the Lord will also love His appearing. That none can be with Christ in any other way, is evident from the whole Bible. The dead are not with Christ, for "the dead praise not the Lord, neither any that go down into silence." Ps. 115:17. "In death there is no remembrance" of the Lord. Ps. 6:5. "The living know that they shall die; but the dead know not anything, neither have they any more a reward; for the memory of them is forgotten. Also their love, and their hatred, and their envy, is now perished." Eccl. 9:5, 6. The old hymn tells us that "death is the gate to endless joy," but the Bible tells us that death is an enemy. 1 Cor. 15:26. Since it is an enemy, we may know that it does not admit us to heaven, and the hymn is false.

Moreover "death came by sin." Rom. 5:12. If it were true that death is the gate to endless joy, then it would follow, since death came by sin, that sin admits men to heaven; but that is so palpably false and unscriptural that no one with any respect for the Bible can hold it. Still further: the devil is the one who has the power of death. Heb. 2:14. Now if death were the way to be with Christ, and the gate of heaven, then we should have the devil as the gate-keeper of heaven! But that is too monstrous for consideration. So we must accept the common-sense Scriptural fact, that death is an enemy, of the human race, and that Christ came to deliver us from it. He came to destroy death, and him that had the power of death. Through the crucifixion and resurrection of Jesus, the power of death, yea, death itself, is destroyed, and Christ's second coming is simply the consummation of Calvary. He comes for the salvation of His people. Isa. 35:4.

We see friends sicken and die. We see them carried, cold and silent, to the grave, and every tear that is shed, and every funeral train and procession of mourners gives the lie to the statement that death is a friend. One may say it as a matter of theology, but when he meets it face to face he gives involuntary testimony to the fact that it is a bitter, cruel enemy. At such times the heathen cannot but break out into wild wailing; for death has no hope in it. But the Christian, while he must sorrow for the loss of loving companionship, cannot sorrow as those who have no hope, for Christ's coming gives hope in death. He will come. This is the comfort of those who mourn. Loved ones who have been separated by death shall thus be united; for at the sound of the trumpet the dead shall be raised incorruptible, then the living, also made immortal, shall be caught up together with them to meet the Lord in the air; and so shall we ever be with the Lord. That is the only way, and that is what makes the promise of Christ's coming such blessed comfort.

Ever with the Lord! Yes, that is the comfort. Friends are to be united at the coming of the Lord, but only the presence of the Lord will make that a joyful meeting. We long for His coming in order that we may be with Him.

He is coming to receive us to Himself. Do not lose sight of that. It is Christ alone who can sanctify all earthly friendships. "Love is of God." Therefore it is only the fact that we shall ever be with the Lord, that will make the meeting with friends a heaven. His presence outshines everything else. Without Him friends would be enemies.

Preparing a Place

"I go to prepare a place for you. And if I go and prepare a place for you, I will come again, and receive you unto Myself, that where I am, there ye may be also." He knows when the place is prepared for His people; we do not. He has said that when the place is prepared He will come for us; we must believe that He will keep His word. Suppose for a moment that we had the power to do as we pleased, and should go to heaven before Christ's second coming; we should find no place ready for us. We should be in the embarrassing position of guests coming before the appointed time. But there is no danger that anybody will be in that position; for we have the assurance of Christ's words, that the only way we can go to be with Him is for Him to come again and take us. Knowing this, all His true disciples will join in the prayer of the beloved disciple: "Come, Lord Jesus."

The Way

Yet we are in danger of making that petition misunderstandingly. We are in danger of forgetting that Christ is the way to the heavenly mansions; that none can attain to the resurrection of the just except those who are "found in Him" at His coming, not having their own righteousness, "but that which is through the faith of Christ, the righteousness which is of God by faith." Phil. 3:9. No man cometh to the Father, to the place where God sits "in light that no man can approach unto," except by Christ, who hath once "suffered for sins, the just for the unjust, that He might bring us to God." 1 Peter 3:18. But in order that we may at the last day and so on throughout eternity be able to stand before God and see His face, we must now draw near. Even now must we dwell in the secret place of the Most High, and full provision for this has been made, for now, even *"now* in Christ Jesus ye who sometimes were far off are made nigh by the blood of Christ." Eph. 2:13. "Through Him we both have access by one Spirit unto the Father." We must come to God and become acquainted with Him before we can see Him; and Christ is the way.

Oh, what depth and breadth of comfort there is in those words of Jesus, "I am the way"! We have all sinned, "all gone out of the way," and know not how to find God. We would gladly return to the Father's house, but we know not the way. Jesus says, "I am the way." His name is Emanuel, God with us, and He is with us all the days, even unto the end of the world, so that although we may wander far from God, behold, the way back to Him is close beside us. Though we wander out of the way, it goes with us, so that even while we may be fleeing from the way, the way is seeking us; for "the Son of man is come to seek and to save that which was lost." Luke 19:10. What a wonderful way is this, that itself seeks the wanderer! How easy it is to find our way back to God!

"I am the way." You do not know how to do that which you would? Jesus is the way. "I have a frightful temper, and don't know how to get the victory over it." "I am the way." Are you overburdened with cares, and know not how to accomplish the tasks that *must* be done? Still Jesus says, "I am the way." Would you learn the best way of doing the work to which you are called, so that you can be "a workman that needeth not to be ashamed?" Jesus is the way. He knows how to do that of which you know nothing; and that which you know how to do well, He knows how to do better. And not only does He know how to do it, so that He can teach you, but He is the way to do it, for He is the life.

The Life

Christ is the life, as well as the way, therefore He is the living way. We cannot get the benefit of Christ as the way, unless we know Him as the life. He is the Word of life, the light of men. "And the Word was made flesh, and dwelt among us." In other words, "the life was manifested, and we have seen it." There is no real life but the life of Christ—Christ Himself. His life—He Himself—is the true light which lighteth every man that cometh into the world. He has forever identified Himself with humanity, that men may forever be made one with Divinity. He has taken all mankind upon Himself, and is the bearer of all the burdens of humanity. His life given freely to every soul, is the way from sin to righteousness. It is the victory.

Altogether too much is Christ kept at a distance. He is near, but men persist in building up barriers which God has broken down. The middle wall of partition between man and God has been broken down and taken away in the flesh of Christ, so that every man may be, if he will, what Christ is. "The Word was made flesh," and He has "abolished in His flesh the enmity," even the fleshly mind. Now He was made our flesh. "There is one kind of flesh of men, another flesh of beasts, another of fishes, another of birds." 1 Cor. 15:39. It was the flesh of men that Christ took. It was the flesh of sinful men too that He took, for He was "made of the seed of David according to the flesh." Rom. 1:4. Yet He "knew no sin." 2 Cor. 5:21. "He was manifested to take away our sins; and in Him is no sin." 1 John 3:5. If therefore we will believe, and acknowledge, and hold to, the truth that Christ is our life, we shall find in reality that "as He is so are we in this world." 1 John 4:17.

"Every spirit that confesseth that Jesus Christ is come in the flesh is of God." 1 John 4:2. "If thou shalt confess with thy mouth the Lord Jesus, and shalt believe in thine heart that God hath raised Him from the dead, thou shalt be saved." Rom. 10:9. How shall we confess the Lord Jesus? What shall we confess about Him?—Confess the truth, namely, that He is come in the flesh, even in our own sinful flesh. Reckon ourselves to be dead, and Him alone to be alive—*the life*. Then will all things be of God, who hath reconciled us to Himself by Jesus Christ. Then it will no longer be we who profess to be living, and bunglingly trying to manage our own affairs, but Christ who actually lives, and who successfully does the will of God in us. The connection between us and Christ must be a vital one, if we would walk in the way. It must not be simply a joining of hands, that He may lead us in the way, but a union of hearts and lives. We must be lost in Him. Remember that *He is the way*; therefore if we would walk in the right way, we must live in Him. The identification between us and Him must be complete. What wondrously glorious possibilities there are for us in the fact that Christ is the way and the life—the living way. Let Him be it, and all will be well.

The Truth

Jesus is the truth. He says, "If ye continue in My Word, then are ye My disciples indeed; and ye shall know the truth, and the truth shall make you free." "If the Son therefore shall set you free, ye shall be free indeed." John 8:31, 32, 36. Thus we see that the Son is the truth which makes free. Only He can give freedom, for nothing but the truth can make men free. Apart from the truth there is only bondage.

"The wrath of God is revealed from heaven against all ungodliness and unrighteousness of men who hold down the truth in unrighteousness." Rom. 1:18, R.V. That is to say that God's wrath is manifested against the ungodliness of those who repress Christ, and refuse to let Him live His perfect life in them. This corroborates the statement that Christ is in every sinful man, ready and anxious to make his life perfect. The fact that a man lives and has breath, which he may use in denying the existence of God, is proof of the presence of God in his flesh. And He is there not to condemn or destroy, but to save. The fact that He stays there and endures all the abuse and shame that is heaped upon Him, proves His forbearance and longsuffering and love. If therefore one will simply "give up," let go of himself, the truth—the life of Christ—will just as surely manifest itself in him, and will be his life, as grain will grow when good seed is sown in the ground. God has made the way of truth so easy and simple that there is no excuse for those who do not walk in it.

Christ is *the truth*. There is no other. There is no truth in the universe that is not true simply because it is some part of the manifestation of Christ. And there is nothing true that is not in Him. Now it is evident that that which is not true does not really exist. We admit this when we say, "It is not so." When God made all these things, He created them by His Word. He said, "Let it be," "and it was so," that is, it came into being. That which is not so has only a fictitious existence. It *seems* to be, but the end will show that it is not. If sought for, it cannot be found. In the Sanskrit, from which our language originates, the word for "truth" means simply "that which is." Christ is; His name is "I AM," and so He is "the truth."

There are men who deny Christ, the truth. How much do such men really know?—Nothing. This is plain enough if we stick to the text. The truth is that which is. But no one can know that which is not. Nobody can know that a thing is so when it is not so. Suppose now, as often happens, that a man has spent a long time diligently studying, and thinks that he has reached a profound conclusion, and it turns out that there is not a word of truth in all that he has been studying. His supposed facts are only fancies. What has he gained? How much does he know as the result of his studies?—Simply nothing. So we see that only in Christ are to be found "all the treasures of wisdom and knowledge." He is the author and perfecter of faith, and only by faith can we understand. That which is, is the thing that hath been, and which will be. Christ is the One "which was, and which is, and which is to come." The truth endures forever, simply because *it is*, and therefore whosoever doeth the truth, or abides in the truth, abides forever. Men may think that they can acquire vast stores of wisdom, and yet deny Christ, that is, deny Him in their lives, deny His right to be their life; but all their seeming knowledge will at the last perish with them, showing that both it and they were in reality nothing. Then will it be demonstrated that only in Christ, in knowing Him, can men know anything. Therefore become acquainted with Christ.

The Word and the Work

"Believest thou not that I am in the Father, and the Father in Me? The words that I speak unto you, I speak not of Myself; but the Father which dwells in Me, He doeth the works." John 14:10. Note the change in expression, showing that the Word is the work. We should naturally expect the sentence to run thus: "The words that I speak unto you, I speak not of Myself; but the

Father which dwelleth in Me, He speaketh them." And that is what Christ really said, for whenever God speaks something is done. "By the Word of the Lord were the heavens made." Ps. 33:6.

Now read John 8:28, and find the counterpart of the verse in our lesson. "When you have lifted up the Son of man, then shall ye know that I am (He), and that I do nothing of Myself; but as My Father hath taught Me, I speak these things." In the first text quoted, we read that Jesus does not speak His own words, but that the Father does the works; in this we read that Jesus does not do the works Himself, but that the Father speaks in Him. Thus we see that the Word and the work of God are one and the same thing. If the Word of God abides in us, then the works of God will be manifested. "This is the work of God, that ye believe on Him whom He hath sent." John 6:29.

Great Works and Greater Works

Here is one of the positive assurances of Jesus, that are specially noted by John: "Verily, verily, I say unto you, He that believeth on Me, the works that I do shall he do also; and greater works than these shall he do; because I go unto My Father." John 14:12. How can this be? Do not ask; for just as no man can by searching find out God, so no man can expect to understand how He works, and so of course no one can hope to know how the works of God are wrought in him. The fact is enough for us. "It is God which worketh in you both to will and to do of His good pleasure." Phil. 2:13. Christ was not a monstrosity, a freak of nature, a unique specimen of humanity, never to be paralleled. No; He is *the Man*." He was sent into the world in order that all might have before them an example of a perfect Man, and as a proof that God can make such men. Only as we arrive at "the measure of the stature of the fullness of Christ," do we come to "a perfect man." Eph. 4:13. God has put into us the same word of reconciliation that was in Christ (2 Cor. 5:19); and as it is the word that works, it follows that the same works will be done by those in whom the Word dwells as were done by Christ. Christ's ministry of reconciliation is committed to us. We are now to appear before the world "in Christ's stead," as witness for Him, that through us the world may believe in the existence of Christ. This being the case, it follows that the same works that He did must be done.

"But we don't see them done now." That makes no difference with the truth of Christ's words. It only shows how little faith there is even in the church. Men have been too slow to understand the wondrous possibilities embraced in the faith of Jesus. When we receive "the Spirit of wisdom and revelation in the knowledge of Him," then we shall "know what is the hope of His calling," and "what is the exceeding greatness of His power to usward who believe according to the working of His mighty power which He wrought in Christ when He raised Him from the dead." Eph. 1:17–20. Why not receive that Spirit now?

But what about the "greater works" than those which Christ did? What are they? and how is it possible for us to do them? To both these questions we can only say that we do not know. Moreover it is not likely that we ever will know. Certainly we shall never know *how* the works are done, for it is only by God's almighty skill that they are wrought. If we cannot know how the least works are done, we certainly cannot know how the greatest are done. We do know that the just will come up to the day of judgment totally unconscious of many good deeds that they have done. Matt. 25:37, 38. What mortal man could endure the knowledge that he was doing greater works than Christ did? If he should think such a thing, the thought itself would lift him up above his Lord and Master, and would ensure his fall. So we must be content and even glad not to know how or what God works in us. The root, buried in the soil, cannot see the glorious fruit that is borne through its faithful ministry, but it works steadily in the place assigned it, content simply *to be* what God will have it; even so it should be with us. Our part is to trust; God is then responsible for results.

"And whatsoever ye shall ask in My name, that will I do, that the Father may be glorified in the Son. If ye shall ask anything in My name, I will do it." John 14:13, 14. A most wonderful promise, and yet a most natural one, when we think what it means to pray in the name of Jesus.

In the first place, it does not mean simply the repetition of the word Jesus. That would be but mockery. In Acts 19:13–16 we have an instance of the uselessness of that. The name of Jesus is not to be used as a charm. There is power in it, but it is not the power of magic.

We are to pray in His name. That is, we are to be in the name, and the name is Himself. We are to come, not in our own name and person, but in the name and Person of Jesus of Nazareth. We are not to personate Him, however. Such a fraud would quickly be detected. No; we are to be left entirely out of the question. We are not worthy to approach the throne of God. People say, "I am so unworthy: I am not fit to come into God's presence." Very well, provision has been made for all such cases. We know that Christ is worthy. "In the day of His flesh" He "offered up prayers and supplications with strong crying and tears unto Him that was able to save Him from death, and was heard." Heb. 5:7. God never turned away the prayer of His only begotten Son, even "in the days of His flesh," when He was clothed with our sinful flesh. Everything that He asked was granted. Let us therefore confess that Jesus Christ is come in the flesh— our flesh. Let us deny ourselves,—deny our own existence,—and acknowledge

Him as the only One who liveth. Then it is "not I, but Christ" who approaches the throne of God. Then the answer to our prayers is assured beforehand; for it was for deliverance from our sins that He prayed. Coming thus in His name, we are as sure of receiving the things that we ask for as He was.

Our sins were upon Him, and they are upon Him still, for He is still in the flesh, and is still praying for us. The burden of the world's sin was upon Him, and from this He prayed to be delivered. So we can leave ourselves out of the question, and be lost in pity for Christ, as we see Him struggling under the load of sin. Then our pity moves us to make an unselfish prayer, "for the sake of Jesus." Oh, that He may be delivered from the oppressive load, and may receive His heart's desire! We make common cause with Him. The prayer is heard. He is delivered. But lo, it was our sin that He bore, and as we prayed for deliverance "for Jesus' sake," that He might be freed, our sin was removed, and deliverance came to us. Thus His victory is our joy. We prayed in His name, and the Father could not but grant the petition. But it is self-evident that no prayer "in the name of Jesus" can ever be selfish.

The name of God is in Christ. Ex. 23:21. So when we pray in the name of Jesus, we are presenting God's own name as the Surety. With what delight then we read the assurance, "Thou shalt not take the name of the Lord thy God in vain." That is a commandment, say you? True; but you must know that in Christ all the commandments of God are blessed promises. Truly, "His commandments are not grievous." "In keeping of them there is great reward."

—April 13, 1899

Chapter 18
The Comforter

John 14:15–27

"If ye love Me, keep My commandments."

Who is there that sees anything severe or arbitrary in this requirement? If there be such an one, it is because he does not know the character of the Lord. Suppose you have a dear friend who is going to a distant land to be gone several years. You are sad at the thought of parting, but he comforts you with the assurance that he will come again, and that then he will remain with you; and then, putting a likeness of himself into your hands, he says, "If you love me, keep this." Would you go about bewailing your hard lot? Would you say that it was asking too much of you? Indeed you would not. On the contrary, you would rejoice at such a token of your friend's love and confidence. Even so should we regard this keepsake from our Lord.

The commandments of Jesus are the commandments of God the Father; for God said of Him to Moses: "I will raise them up a Prophet from among their brethren, like unto thee, and will put My words in His mouth; and He shall speak unto them all that I shall command Him. And it shall come to pass, that whosoever will not hearken unto My words which He shall speak in My name, I will require it of him." Deut. 17:18, 19. Jesus said: "I have not spoken of Myself; but the Father which sent Me, He gave Me a commandment, what I should say, and what I should speak. Whatsoever I speak therefore, even as the Father said unto Me, so I speak." John 12:49, 50. He was simply the revelation of God to men, the manifestation of God in the flesh, so that it was God speaking in Him. The law of God was in His heart (Ps. 40:8), so that He was that law personified.

Jesus is the One who gives freedom. John 8:34–36. The law of the Spirit of life in Christ Jesus gives freedom from sin and death. Rom. 8:2. He therefore is the "perfect law of liberty" into which we are to look as into a mirror, beholding not our own sinful selves, but "the image of the invisible God," into whose image we are transformed as we behold. James 1:25; Col. 1:15; 2 Cor. 3:18.

Therefore in requiring us to keep His commandments, He simply asks us to keep a memorial of Himself. Love will gladly do this. "This is the love of God, that we keep His commandments; and His commandments are not grievous."

"He that hath My commandments, and keepeth them, he it is that loveth Me."

When God made man, the crown and lord of creation, He planted a garden eastward in Eden; "and the Lord God took the man, and put him into the garden of Eden, to dress it and to keep it." Gen. 2:8, 15. Man did not have to make the garden; he was not required to plant it; he was only to dress it and to keep it. God made it perfect; man's duty was only to keep that which God had committed to him. So God gives us His commandments, His own perfect righteousness, and asks us to keep it. By faith in God we keep the commandments; so that one has only to keep the faith in order to keep God's commandments. To us all, even as to Timothy, comes the exhortation, "Keep that which is committed to thy trust." It should not be considered a hardship to keep what is given to us, when that thing is the highest good.

Notice that this talk about keeping the commandments immediately follows the promise that if we shall ask anything in His name He will do it. "And whatsoever we ask, we receive of Him, because we keep His commandments, and do those things that are pleasing in His sight. And this is His commandment, that we should believe on the name of His Son Jesus Christ, and love one another." 1 John 3:22, 23. "Love is the fulfilling of the law," and love is freely shed abroad in our hearts by the Holy Spirit. He makes the conditions of answered prayer very easy, and then supplies the conditions.

"And I will pray the Father, and He shall give you another Comforter, that He may abide with you forever; even the Spirit of truth; whom the world cannot receive, because it seeth Him not, neither knoweth Him; but ye know Him; for He dwelleth in you, and shall be in you. I will not leave you comfortless [orphans]: I will come to you." John 14:16–18.

Jesus Himself is a Comforter. His presence is comfort. It was because He was going away, that the hearts of the disciples were troubled; and Jesus comforted them with the assurance that He was going to the Father, to prepare a place for them. Therefore we may know that "if any man sin, we have a Comforter with the Father, Jesus Christ the righteous." 1 John 2:1. The word rendered "Advocate," in this text is identical with that rendered "Comforter" in John 14:16. We have a Comforter with the Father, and "another Comforter" on earth with us. Surely we have no lack of comfort.

This Comforter, the Spirit of truth, is Christ's own representative, Christ's own personal presence with us as He could not be in the flesh. We know this in two ways from our text. First, Jesus says, "I will send you another Comforter," and adds, "I will not leave you orphans; I will come to you." So through the Spirit Christ is personally present even when absent. If, when talking to Nicodemus, He could speak of Himself as "the Son of man, which is in heaven" (John 3:13), now that He is on the right hand of God in the heavens He may with equal truth speak of Himself as with us.

In the second place, we know that the Spirit is but Christ's larger presence, so to speak, because the Comforter is "the Spirit of truth." Jesus Christ is "the truth." John 14:6. The Spirit of truth therefore is Christ's very essence. Having the Spirit, we have Christ and all that He possesses.

"I will not leave you orphans." Christ is "the Everlasting Father" (Isa. 9:6), and He is the living image of the Father, the shining of His glory. Therefore the Holy Spirit, Christ's representative, who brings Christ's own presence, brings also the presence of the Father, so that with Him we are not orphans. Through the Spirit we become sons of God, members of His household, and the Father Himself is with us all the time. No longer are we prodigal wanderers from our Father's house, but sharers of all His bounty.

The world cannot receive the Spirit, because it cannot see Him. The world's motto is, "Seeing is believing;" the truth is that "believing is seeing." The world does not believe, and so it does not really see; it only imagines. It is not content with a God whom it cannot see, and therefore it manufactures gods. Out of its own imagination it makes images, and worships them. The Spirit, however, can be received only by faith, and whoever believes endures as seeing the invisible. All who believe may know the presence and voice of the Holy Spirit just as surely as they may know their most intimate friends, and even more so, since they can have no other friend so intimate. "Ye know Him; for He dwelleth with you, and shall be in you." Do you ask how you will know Him? Believe and you will know for yourself, as no one can tell you.

"Yet a little while, and the world seeth Me no more; but ye see Me; because I live, ye shall live also." Christ is our life, and the fact that we live is proof of His presence. "But the wicked live!" you exclaim. Yes, and that proves the grace and mercy of God; it shows His presence to save. The Spirit of life and righteousness is striving with all, seeking to be received as a welcomed guest. Christ says to His true disciples, "Ye see Me." This is true even now that He is absent so that the world cannot see Him. But He is present now only by the Holy Spirit, which proves that believers have ocular demonstration of the presence of the Spirit. Yes, faith enables men to see spiritual things.

"He shall teach you all things." There is no teacher like God (Job 36:22), for "out of His mouth cometh knowledge and understanding." Prov. 2:6. The Holy Spirit is "the Spirit of wisdom and understanding, the Spirit of counsel and might, the Spirit of knowledge and the fear of the Lord." Isa. 11:2. He is "the Spirit of wisdom and revelation in the knowledge of God." His very presence gives wisdom. Through the Spirit one knows things that without Him could never be learned by any amount of study.

Without the Spirit, one really knows nothing. This is a fact. See: The Spirit is bestowed in order that we may know the things that are freely given to us by God. 1 Cor. 2:12. Since God does nothing uselessly, it is evident that without the Spirit we could not know the things that God freely gives us. Now what does He give us?—With His Son He freely gives us all things. Rom. 8:32. There is nothing that God does not give us, and nothing of that which He gives us can be known without the Spirit; therefore without the Spirit we cannot really know anything. The school of Christ—the school of meekness and humility—is the school in which true knowledge of even the most common things is obtained, and the reception of the Spirit ensures to us the highest education.

Think a moment, and you will see that this is literally true. Take two men, one having all the advantages of the best schools in the land, and the other compelled to spend all his life in hard, manual labour. The one will have all the polish that the world can give, while the other may present a rougher exterior, and may not be able to pass even an entrance examination in schools from which the first has been graduated with honour. The one is a skeptic, while the other knows and fears the Lord, and has obtained the wisdom that comes from above. James 3:17. Which one has the advantage in education? You may hastily say, the first. Not so fast. Remember that this whole life, even though it be fourscore years, is but the threshold of eternity, and you must never leave eternity out of your reckoning. The Judgment comes, and the first goes to destruction, and all his attainments perish with him, while the other has before him endless ages of association with God and angels, whose acquaintance he has made on earth. Say you not that even the very first day of the life beyond, the poor man knows more than the other? When you first judged, you were like one who should make his decision as to two men upon their entrance to school. The end is the time to pass judgment. None of this that has been said by any means depreciates learning or application; far from it; for the one who knows the Lord will by that very companionship be stimulated to reach out forevery attainable thing, and will be enabled to make more advancement in solid knowledge than an unbeliever can.

"He shall teach you all things." The Spirit is the only teacher. Whatever one learns from any other person he does not really know. "Ye have an unction from the Holy One, and ye know all things." 1 John 2:20. "The anointing which ye have received of Him abideth in you, and ye need not that any man teach you; but as the same anointing teacheth you of all things, and is truth, and is no lie, and even as it hath taught you, ye shall abide in Him." Verse 27. No one is to learn of man. It is true that God has set teachers in the church, and He uses men as agents for conveying instruction; but the one who receives the instruction as coming from man, instead of direct from God, does not know the truth. No matter by whom the instruction comes, unless the learner receives it so directly from the Spirit that he knows it as a personal revelation from God, he does not have it as he ought to have it.

"The Comforter, which is the Holy Ghost, ... shall bring all things to your remembrance, whatsoever I have said unto you." Since all things that are worth remembering come from Christ alone, and the Spirit brings them all to our remembrance, when we receive Him, it follows that the Spirit is given to us to be memory for us. Mind, the Spirit is not a substitute for study and application, and is not given to encourage laziness; but He is our Teacher, spurring us on, and helping us, and becoming so one with us that He takes complete possession, so that we have no mind but that of the Spirit. Then the Spirit is understanding, and memory as well, enabling us to think of the right thing at just the right time.

The Declaration of Peace

"Peace I leave with you, My peace I give unto you; not as the world giveth, give I unto you. Let not your heart be troubled, neither let it be afraid."

So the chapter ends where it began. "Let not your heart be troubled." Peace is ours, then how can we be troubled. Do not get things reversed. We are not to believe that we have peace because we have no trouble; but since Christ has given us His peace, we are not to be troubled, no matter how great the trouble.

"My peace I give unto you." Peace, perfect peace, means victory. In that Christ gives us His peace, He gives us His victory. He has conquered, and put the enemy to flight, after taking from him all his armour wherein he trusted, and He gives us peace. Not only so, but He gives us *His peace*—the peace that was unruffled even in the fiercest fight. He was oppressed and persecuted as no other man ever was; spies were continually on His track, perverting His words, seeking to exasperate Him, whispering about Him, bearing false witness, defaming His character, arousing suspicion, contradicting and abusing Him; yet never once was He impatient. What perfect peace! And this peace He has given us. We are not able to keep patient under trials, but the peace of Jesus can keep us. "Be careful for nothing; but in everything by prayer and supplication with thanksgiving let your requests be made known unto God. And the peace of God, which passeth all understanding, shall keep your hearts and minds through Christ Jesus." Phil. 4:6, 7.

—April 20, 1899

Chapter 19

The Vine and the Branches

John 15:1–14

"I am the true vine, and My Father is the husbandman. Every branch in Me that beareth not fruit He taketh away, and every branch that beareth fruit He purgeth it, that it may bring forth more fruit. Now ye are clean through the word which I have spoken unto you. Abide in Me, and I in you. As the branch cannot bear fruit of itself, except it abide in the vine; no more can ye, except ye abide in Me. I am the vine, ye are the branches. He that abideth in Me, and I in him, the same bringeth forth much fruit."

The passover supper had been eaten. Jesus had performed the last loving act of humble service for His disciples, the closing hymn had been sung, and now they were on their way to the garden that was to be the scene of the Saviour's greatest struggle with the powers of darkness. Nothing is more common than a vine forming an arbour; and Jesus, who was always ready to impress a lesson by the things that were before Him, took advantage of the sight of a vine that they passed to teach His disciples an important lesson on the reality of things. He would have them know that the things that are seen are temporal, but the things that are unseen are real and eternal (2 Cor. 4:18), so that they might endure "as seeing Him who is invisible."

Jesus is the *true* vine. All vines that we see growing out of the earth, and bearing fruit, are but visible proofs of the presence of the invisible vine—the reality. The seed of everything that grows is the Word of God. Luke 8:11. In the beginning, when the earth was first created, and there was nothing in it, God said, "Let the earth bring forth grass, the herb yielding seed, and the fruit tree yielding fruit after his kind. Gen. 1:11. "And it was so." God's word was the seed whence every plant of every kind sprung. Just as He sent His word out into darkness, and light shone forth, so He sent His word into the vacant earth, and vegetation appeared. But Jesus is "the Word of God." "In the beginning was the Word, and the Word was with God, and the Word was God… All things were made by Him." John 1:13. Hence Christ is the Seed. This is true in the most comprehensive sense. Our confidence in Him as the righteous seed that shall beget righteousness in us, is made perfect by seeing the efficient working of that seed in all creation. "The Word was made flesh" dwelling among us "full of grace and truth;" and the possibility of this is shown to us, even before we experience it, by the fact, seen everywhere, that the word was made grass, herbs, and trees. The life that is able to bring the vegetable creation to perfection, is also able to make our way perfect, when it is given free course.

Evidence of the truth of the statement that Christ is the true vine was given at the very beginning of His ministry. At the wedding in Cana Jesus turned the water into wine. Water was put into the jars, and wine was drawn out. The same miracle is wrought every year. Water falls from heaven upon the ground, and is drawn up into the vine, and comes out wine. The miracle wrought in Cana was for the purpose of letting us know that every particle of water that is turned to wine in all the vines on earth, is changed only by the presence and power of Christ, the true vine.

The water that makes the earth fruitful is the water of life from the river of God. Ps. 65:9–11. The water comes from the slain Lamb in the midst of the throne (Rev. 5:6; 7:17), just as the water which the Israelites drank in the desert came from Christ. 1 Cor. 10:4. The Spirit of God is the water of life (John 7:37–39), and the Spirit and the water and the blood agree in one. 1 John 5:8. This is shown by the water and the blood that flowed from the pierced side of Christ as He hung on the cross. John 19:34, 35. The blood is the life. Thus we see that when Jesus gave "the fruit of the vine" to His disciples at the last supper, He stated the literal truth when He said, "This is My blood." The fruit of the vine, which refreshes man, imparting to him life, is the blood of Christ, the true vine!

But this is not all. We can never exhaust the wonder that Christ is the real vine; but more wonderful still to our comprehension is the fact that we are the branches, and as such are to bear fruit. It is the branches that bear the fruit. This is no cause for boasting, for it is the vine that bears the branches, and the branches produce nothing, but are wholly dependent on the parent stock; but when they are joined to the vine by a vital connection they bear the fruit. "Ye have not chosen Me, but I have chosen you, and ordained you, that ye should go and bring forth fruit, and that your fruit should remain." John 15:16.

From this we see that Christ expects us to do the work that is done on this earth, or, rather, that He expects the work to be done through us. He Himself said, "I can of Mine own self do nothing." John 5:30. "The Father that dwelleth in Me, He doeth the works." John 14:10. So the "miracles and wonders and signs" were what "God did by Him." Acts. 2:22. So we can do nothing apart from Him. He is the motive power, and we are the ones in whom the results are to be seen, and the fruit that is seen is counted to us as ours. God has placed us here in this world instead of Christ, who is with the Father. The Father is the keeper of the vineyard whose root and stock are in heaven, and the branches on the earth.

"Herein is My Father glorified, that ye bear much fruit." The fruit borne is "the fruit of the light." Eph. 5:9, R.V. Therefore we are exhorted, "Let your light so shine before men, that they may see your good works, and glorify your Father which is in heaven." Matt. 5:16. The last message that goes forth,—the last proclamation of the Gospel, which announces the hour of God's Judgment already come,—is a message exhorting to fruit-bearing, in these words: "Fear God, and give glory to Him; for the hour of His Judgment is come; and worship Him that made heaven, and earth, and the sea, and the fountains of waters." Rev. 14:6, 7. God is glorified by us only as we bring forth fruit; and it is by His power that is manifest in all creation, that we are to do this.

Thus it is that the last message to mankind calls special attention to God as Creator. When the Lord comes His glory is to cover the heavens, uniting with the glory that fills the earth. The glory of the Lord is to be revealed so that all flesh can see it together before the Lord comes. Isa. 40:3–5. The cry, "Behold your God!" will be sounded in the ears of all, and they will be directed to the things that He has made in order to see it. Rom. 1:18–20. When they see Him working in the rest of creation, those who wish to bring forth fruit to the glory of God will be convinced that He is able to work as mightily in them, to cause them to bring forth the fruit for which He created them.

But in spite of the fact that that which may be known of God is manifest in all men, and that the invisible things of Him, even His everlasting power and Divinity, are clearly revealed in the things that He has made, people are apt to get so absorbed in themselves that they will walk in the midst of the revelations of God's life and power as though they were blind. Therefore God has given us a memorial of Himself, that His wonderful works, and so He Himself, may be remembered. Ps. 111:2–4. He says, "I gave them My Sabbaths, to be a sign between me and them, that they might know that I am the Lord that sanctify them." Eze. 20:12. This memorial endures to all generations. Week by week the Sabbath calls our attention anew to the fact that God is the Creator of all things, and that He creates all things very good. Thus we are continually reminded to put our trust in Him for salvation. He is the husbandman, and He keeps His vineyard day and night, watering it every moment. Isa. 27:2, 3.

Friends of the Lord

"Ye are My friends, if ye do whatsoever I command you." And what does He command us?—To bear fruit. Strange that immediately after reading the first part of this chapter, in which the conditions of fruit-bearing are so clearly set forth, and it is shown that we ourselves do nothing of ourselves, but simply bear the fruit which the life of the parent stock begets in us, men will read this fourteenth verse, and imagine that they must by their own power to do something to recommend them to the Lord, and gain His friendship! "This is the work of God, that ye believe in Him whom He hath sent." John 6:29. His commandment to us is fulfilled by our trust in Him; "even as Abraham believed God, and it was accounted to him for righteousness." Gal. 3:6.

Without faith it is impossible to please God. Abraham our father was justified by works when he had offered up Isaac his son upon the altar, because "faith wrought with his works, and by works was faith made perfect. And the Scripture was fulfilled which saith, Abraham believed God, and it was imputed unto him for righteousness; and he was called the Friend of God." James. 2:21-23. God was Abraham's friend before this, but Abraham thus became God's friend. God is the Friend of all men, the Friend of sinners; but the sad fact is that very few will consent to be friendly with God. They have no confidence in Him.

"The friendship of the Lord is with them that fear Him; and He will show them His covenant." Ps. 25:14, R.V., margin. As other versions have it, God's confidential association is with them that fear Him. To such He makes known secrets about Himself, that only those can know who come close enough to Him for Him to whisper in their ears.

Friendship must be mutual. Friends exchange confidences. Jesus says: "I have called you friends; for all things that I have heard of My Father I have made known unto you." Whoever has friends must show himself friendly. If we wish to retain the friendship of God, and have a share in His secrets, we must not withhold from Him anything concerning ourselves. We must not have any secrets from Him. We must tell Him all, confessing all our sins. Not that He does not already know them, but this is the proof of our friendship. Then He reveals to us the secret of His salvation. "If we confess our sins, He is faithful and just to forgive us our sins, and to cleanse us from all unrighteousness." 1 John 1:9. He will not betray our confidence. No; not only will He conceal our sins from public gaze at the last day, casting them into the depths of the sea, so that although they are sought for by our adversary the devil, the accuser, they cannot be found (Jer. 50:20), but even He Himself will forget them. Heb. 8:12. What a wonderful inducement to make friends with God! Delay not; for now is the accepted time; now is the day of salvation.

—April 27, 1899

Chapter 20
The Wondrous Name

John 18:1–14

Christ Betrayed and Arrested

Two texts of scripture may be taken as the key to the portion before us in this week's study. They are John 14:30, "The prince of this world cometh, and hath nothing in Me," and John 13:1, "Having loved His own which were in the world, He loved them unto the end," or "to the uttermost."

Jesus had finished His last confidential talk with His disciples. It had been confidential indeed, as none other could ever have been, for the presence of the traitor was not there. Jesus had treated Judas just as He had the other disciples, so that not one of them had any idea of his true character; yet it was impossible that there should have been that close fellowship between him and the Master that there was with the others. Judas was continually repelling the Master and His instruction, while the others, faulty as they were, were receptive.

Very tender had the words of Jesus been. He had addressed them as "little children," and had made the most comforting promises to them. Now He led them to the familiar spot where He had so often resorted with them.

"And Judas also, which betrayed Him, knew the place." There was no attempt at concealment on the part of Christ. He would not hide. He did not do anything to court betrayal and persecution, but proceeded just as He had many times before. In sight of the cross the actions of Jesus were as calm and dignified as ever. The grandeur and dignity and authority, yea, the Kingliness, of the Man stand out this last night more clearly than ever before.

"Judas then, having received a band of men and officers from the chief priests and Pharisees, cometh thither with lanterns and torches and weapons. Jesus therefore, knowing all things that should come upon Him, went forth, and said unto them, Whom seek ye?"

Think of it! A band of soldiers with weapons, going forth to capture a single unarmed man, who had never harmed a living creature, and who would not fight even in self-defense. Guilty consciences they all must have had, which made cowards of them. But strong as their force of men was, it was altogether too small and weak to accomplish their purpose, if it had been a contest of strength. Jesus was led as a lamb to the slaughter. He was the Lamb of God, bearing the sins of the world; but the world knew it not. Men do not arm themselves with weapons to capture a single lamb.

And now see Jesus stand forth before that armed mob. "Whom seek ye?" A pertinent question, truly. Whom should they be seeking in that place, in such a manner? The question should have put every man of them to shame, but they were not ashamed. Boldly they answered, "Jesus of Nazareth." Who is He, whom this armed crowd are seeking as though He were a fierce desperado? It is Jesus of Nazareth, the gentle Being who had all His life gone about doing good, healing the sick, relieving the oppressed, and comforting the mourners. His tender touch had nothing but healing in it, for He came to save life, not to take. And now they come for Him as though it were a bear they were after. In this foolish and unnecessary precaution, and in the calm boldness of Jesus, we see a fulfillment of the scripture; "The wicked flee when no man pursueth; but the righteous are bold as a lion." Prov. 28:1.

"I Am"

To the question, "Whom seek ye?" the leaders of the mob answered, "Jesus of Nazareth;" to which Jesus replied, "I am *He*." "As soon as He had said unto them, I am *He*, they went backward, and fell to the ground."

What marvelous power there was in those few words! Perhaps the mystery will be clearer if we consider closely what it was that Jesus really said. Notice that the word "He" is in Italic, indicating that it is an addition to the text. Christ's own words, as recorded in the Greek, are simply, "I am." To Moses in the wilderness, the Lord had said of this name, "This is My name forever, and this is My memorial unto all generations." Ex. 3:14, 15. By this name Jesus had declared Himself to the unbelieving Jews. John 8:24, 28, 58. The time had now come, of which He had said, "When ye have lifted up the Son of man, then shall ye know that I am." In the very hour of His betrayal, and to His persecutors, He revealed Himself by that glorious name by which He delivered the children of Israel from bondage, and by which He delivers all who trust in it. In His answer to them, in making Himself known as the One whom they were seeking to put to death, Jesus revealed Himself to them as their Saviour. But they were then too blinded to receive the revelation. No evidence could affect them then, but afterwards some of the very ones who had been His betrayers and murderers found peace in believing on the I AM—the Author of life.

Power of the Name

There is wondrous power in this blest name. When Jesus came to His disciples in that stormy night on the sea, when they were tired with rowing against terrible odds, and were despairing of life, He brought courage and salvation to them by the word, "Be of good cheer; I am, be not afraid." Matt. 14:27. That same name was in this trying hour a protection to His loved disciples. As soon as He had uttered it, the armed crowd went backward, and fell to the ground as if struck down by invisible weapons. Here was evidence of the Divinity of Christ, which should have caused those men to desist from their purpose. The power of Christ was manifested on this occasion no less for the salvation of His enemies than for His disciples.

Christ's own name was as a shield round about Him. It was an impenetrable wall, effectually protecting Him from all foes. "The prince of this world" could find no access to Him. He had nothing in Him, and therefore there was no pretext upon which He could enter. By the utterance of that name Jesus showed that no man or men could deprive Him of life, but that He Himself gave it up willingly.

That very name, with the same protecting power, is ours to take with us. That little incident in the garden is recorded in order that we may know that the I AM, who is with us all the days, even to the end of the world, is our shield against all the assaults of the enemy of our souls. He puts His own name upon us. Into that name we are baptized. While we confess that name, knowing that Christ is come in our flesh, and that it is no longer we who live and have to meet the attacks of Satan, but Christ living in us, we can as certainly keep the roaring lion at bay as Jesus did the fierce mob. What a blessed lesson is conveyed to us in this simple narrative!

> "Take the name of Jesus ever,
> As a shield from every snare;
> When temptations round you gather,
> Breathe that holy name in prayer."

Saving to the Uttermost

"Of them which Thou gavest me have I lost none." By the manifestation of His power through the utterance of the words, "I am," Jesus secured the safety of His disciples. "He loved them unto the end." Here we see proof that the name of Jesus is a protection. Not, however, when used merely as a charm. "The name of the Lord is a strong tower; the righteous runneth into it, and is safe." Prov. 18:10. It must be known as a real thing, in which the soul lives, in order for it to be a protection. Some men who did not know the Lord once attempted to use His name for their own selfish interests, and the result was most disastrous to them. See Acts 19:13–16.

In all His trial, Jesus never lost sight of His disciples. His care was for them, not for Himself. He knew all things that should come upon Him, yet not for a moment was He terrified. He came to save others by the sacrifice of Himself, and not once did He forget His mission. A soul less firm than the "Rock of Ages" would have been disconcerted and thrown off his balance. But Jesus was as calm as when sitting in the house of Lazarus. In the hour of greatest trial He demonstrated His power to keep all those who flee to Him for refuge.

A Protest Against War

"Then Simon Peter having a sword, drew it, and smote the high priest's servant, and cut off his right ear. The servant's name was Malchus. Then said Jesus unto Peter, Put up thy sword into the sheath; the cup which My Father hath given Me, shall I not drink it?"

Jesus had said to His disciples, and to us as well, "I say unto you, That ye resist not evil," and here He showed that His words are to be taken in their plainest signification. If there was ever a place in the world when right was oppressed by might, here it was. If ever in this world the sword was drawn in a just cause, this was the time; yet Jesus rebuked it. Nothing else can be learned from this occurrence than that there are no possible circumstances under which it is justifiable to use weapons of warfare. Such sentiments as the following we find given very frequent and prominent place in religious journals:

> In the last resort,—when insult has been wantonly inflicted, when the obligations of honour have been willfully repudiated, and when every resource of peaceful diplomacy has been exhausted,—no self-respecting nation will be found unprepared to maintain its dignity and enforce its rights by appeal to arms.

Let that serve for those nations and peoples who have no other method of maintaining their honour and dignity than that which is common to the brutes. Jesus showed that there is a better way to maintain one's dignity. He was insulted and abused, yet never did the native dignity of His character assert itself and shine forth more conspicuously, and so victoriously, too, than when He reproved Peter for using the sword. Unarmed, He stood before that crowd of armed men, and demonstrated Himself to be their Master. Every Christian who is such indeed, has the same armour that He had. Read Eph. 6:13. For professed Christians, therefore, to take the sword in self-defense, or for any other purpose, is to admit that they know nothing of "the power of Jesus' name."

Love Your Enemies

In His instruction to His disciples Jesus had also said, "Love your enemies, bless them that curse you, do good to them that hate you." Matt. 5:44. Here He gave a practical illustration of that teaching also. Not only did He reprove Peter for his act of violence to the high priest's servant, but He again showed that He came to save, and not to destroy. He was already in the hands of the mob (Mark 14:46, 47), when the wound was inflicted by the zealous Peter, but He gently disengaged one hand, at the same time courteously saying, as if apologizing for seeming to resist them even to do them a kindness, "Suffer ye thus far," and touched the servant's ear, and healed him. Could Divine kindness be more strikingly manifested? Truly, this Man was the Saviour of the world.

Here we may well rest and contemplate. It is but a brief narrative that we have been studying, but it shines with Divine light. Only one thing more need be said, and that is, "Consider Him that endured such contradiction of sinners against Himself, lest ye be wearied and faint in your minds." Heb. 12:3.

—May 4, 1899

Chapter 21
Denying the Lord

John 18:15–27

Jesus had suffered Himself to be taken by the armed mob which Judas had conducted, and was by them bound and led away to the mock trial. The disciples had protested that nothing could induce them to leave Him; but this was because they did not know what was coming. They were sure that they would not forsake the One who had so tenderly cared for them, and yet had showed Himself so mighty to deliver. They could not conceive of Him in any other state than as they had seen Him going about scattering blessings everywhere, except as they thought of Him taking the kingdom to Himself, driving out the Romans, correcting the abuses that had crept into the Jewish priesthood, and reigning in pomp and majesty. But now they saw Him bound and led away unresistingly; and although they had witnessed the power of the simple words "I AM" which He uttered, they could not hold out against the overwhelming shock of His capture, and "they forsook Him and fled." Mark 14:50.

Even Peter who had been most zealous in his protestation of loyalty to the Master, and who had been valiant enough with the sword, could not keep his courage in the face of the Master's apparent defeat, and he fled with the rest; but when he found that the mob was content with Jesus, that it was the Shepherd and not the sheep they were after, he turned round and "followed afar off." Luke 22:54.

We may be sure that it was not mere curiosity that prompted Peter to follow. He had intense love for Jesus, even as had the other disciples. True, they had not yet attained to that perfect love that casteth out all fear, but they loved Him nevertheless, even though they fled in terror.

John was an acquaintance of the high priest, and so found ready access to the palace. Peter was stopped at the door, but through the influence of John was admitted. As he passed in, the girl that kept the door recognized him, or thought she did, and said, "Art thou not one of this man's disciples?" Peter said, "I am not."

Peter's love for the Master caused him to desire to be as near Him as possible, for he was anxious to see what the outcome would be. Yet it was a perilous time, and he would not endanger himself by seeming to be very much interested in the affair. So he joined the group of servants and officers who stood round the fire, warming themselves, "and Peter stood with them warming himself."

It is not difficult to picture ourselves the state of Peter's mind. Intensely fearful for his own safety, yet anxious about Jesus, compelled by fear to seem to be one of the indifferent crowd about the fire, listening to their rough jokes and loose gossip, which he could not have joined in even if his mind had not been distracted by anxious thought for the Master, and under the necessity of seeming to share in the conversation in which he had no interest and took no part, at the same time straining his ears to hear what passed between Jesus and His merciless persecutors. It was no pleasant position in which he found himself. It is never an easy thing to act a double part, and the circumstances in this case made it doubly trying. Besides, Peter was not hypocritical by nature, but blunt and outspoken. It was his fear that was swaying him now.

But Peter could not succeed in concealing his identity. Indeed, it is most likely that his very efforts to do so made it the more difficult. He was not one of the unfeeling crowd, and could not make himself appear so. He was ill at ease. He could not conceal the deep feeling that he had, and his uneasiness could not but draw the attention of the others to him as he "stood and warmed himself." "They said therefore unto him, Art thou not also one of His disciples? He denied it and said, I am not." Verse 25. This was the second positive denial of Christ that evening.

This, however, was not the end. The very words in which Peter denied the Lord, served to mark him as one of His disciples. Jesus was known as the prophet from Galilee, and His disciples were also Galileans, who spoke with an accent noticeably different from that of the dwellers in Judea and Jerusalem. So "they that stood by said again to Peter, Surely thou art one of them, for thou art a Galilean, and thy speech agreeth thereto." But the more he denied, the more was attention fastened upon him. And "one of the servants of the high priest, being his kinsman whose ear Peter cut off, saith, Did not I see thee in the garden with Him?" John 18:26.

This was bringing Peter into close quarters. He was not only in danger because of his connection with Jesus, but he was likely to suffer because of his rash zeal in the garden. The relative of the wounded man might be inclined to take revenge, if the act were settled upon Peter. And so doubly frightened Peter began to curse and swear, saying, "I know not this man of whom you speak." Mark 14:71. Alas, what a change was this from the loyal Peter in the upper chamber in loving communion with Jesus a few hours before.

All this is recorded for our learning; but unfortunately we too often miss the lesson. It is easier to censure Peter's cowardice than to avoid it. Peter is not the only disciple who has denied his Lord. In fact, the flight of the eleven when Jesus was bound, was in itself a tacit denial of Him. Peter's denial was more marked than that of the rest, but this was but the natural recoil from his boastful possession of faithfulness: "Though all men should be caused to stumble because of Thee, yet will I never be caused to stumble." Matt. 26:33. (See margin of revision.)

Moreover Peter's use of the sword tended to his discomfiture. If he had not used violence, he would have had no special cause for fear. Men are often applauded for bravery which they show in defending the right, or what they conceive to be right, with weapons of war. But that sort of defense, however zealously conducted, may be in reality only a manifestation of cowardice. It requires much more bravery quietly to suffer than fiercely to repel assault. Quiet endurance of injury is a far better expression of real zeal for Christ than are loud professions and vigorous blows.

There is a truth here that needs special emphasis at this time. Would that every Christian gathering might have this lesson strongly set before them. There is scarcely a meeting without resolutions denouncing this or that evil. Religious leaders become almost frenzied in their passionate denunciation of men and measures which they think, and which may really be, opposed to Christ and Christianity. They vie with one another in strong expressions of loyalty to Christianity, and hatred of evil doing; yet when the test comes to them personally to suffer alone and unknown for the truth's sake, too often they are ready to compromise. It is well to speak boldly for truth, but it is better to hold to the truth and say nothing, than to use strong language for it and not live it.

In Titus 1:16, we read of some "who profess that they know God, but in works they deny Him." This is done every time a professed follower of Christ does that which is inconsistent with the character of Christ. "As many of you as have been baptized into Christ, have put on Christ." Gal. 3:27. Whether one has had the reality of this experience or not, the act of baptism indicates that one surrenders himself to Christ; yea, more than this, that he lays down his own life, and takes the life of Christ, so that it is no longer he, but Christ who lives and walks about among men. The old man is declared to be dead, and the new man who takes his place is the Man Christ Jesus. So he calls himself by the name of Christ—a Christian. Now so long as he professes to be a Christian, he says by everything which he does, "This is the way Christ does; this is Christ's character." But if he does those things which are inconsistent with the character of Jesus of Nazareth, then he is denying Him as surely as Peter did, and his guilt may be even greater than was Peter's.

One may deny Christ by his association with others, even though he utter not a word. Peter's mingling with the rude, unfeeling crowd in the court room was in itself a denial of Christ. Not that it was wrong to associate with sinners: this Jesus Himself did; he went in with publicans and sinners and ate with them. But it must be remembered that when Jesus associated with sinners, He did not try to make it appear that He was one of them. He associated with them to win them by His kindness and His example to a better life. And although His demeanor was such that they could associate with Him familiarly, yet when He most appeared to be one with them, there was always apparent the fact that He was far different from them. To stand in the crowd, or sit in the assembly where the rude jest and the coarse talk, and possibly the reviling of that which is good and pure, show that they are the enemies of Christ, is to deny Him, even though one say not a word. Unless one's very presence is a rebuke to sin, it is a countenancing of it: and that is a denial of Christ. "Blessed is the man that walketh not in the counsel of the ungodly, nor standeth in the way of sinners, nor sitteth in the seat of the scornful. But his delight is in the law of the Lord, and in His law doth he meditate day and night."

It was the offence of the cross that caused the disciples to flee, and Peter to deny his Lord. It was not that they loved Christ any the less, but because they were unexpectedly brought face to face with a condition which they had not calculated upon. They had not taken the shame of the cross into consideration when they followed Christ. Jesus had told them of it repeatedly, in order that they might be prepared for this very time, but they had not comprehended His words. They had not counted the cost. They had been willing to accept Jesus as King, even though He was in poverty, and was hated and rejected by the priests and elders, because His power was visibly manifested before them. But they had not learned that God chooses things that are not to bring to naught things that are. So when Jesus seemed to have no power at all in the hands of the mob and on the cross, they failed.

If we would not make the same failure, we must make provision for the cross in our lives. We must not expect that since to be a Christian is to have a name greater than that of the kings of the earth, we shall therefore always be held in high esteem because of our profession. We must remember that the world is in deadly opposition to Christ, and that the world never becomes converted. "Whosoever, therefore, will be a friend of the world is the enemy of God." James 4:4. There can, therefore, be no more positive denial of Christ, than to be like the world, or to seem to be like the world. "Be not conformed to this world, but be ye transformed by the renewing of your mind." Rom. 12:2. Know that that which is highly esteemed by the world is an abomination to the Lord; and that "the base things of the world, and things which are despised hath God chosen." 1 Cor. 1:28. The cross of Christ, which the world looks upon with scorn, is the power of God. Therefore "think it not strange concerning the fiery trial that is to try you, as though some strange thing happened to you; but rejoice inasmuch as ye are partakers of Christ's sufferings." 1 Peter 4:12. Confession of Christ means nonconformity to the world; and those who confess Him in His humiliation will be acknowledged by Him when He comes in His glory. Therefore let our sincere prayer be, "God forbid that I should glory, save in the cross of our Lord Jesus Christ, by whom the world is crucified unto me, and I unto the world."

—May 11, 1899

Chapter 22
The King Before the Judgment Bar

John 18:28–40

A careful study of all the lessons set forth in this portion of Scripture would require many articles. We must therefore ask the reader carefully to study the text indicated, and will content ourselves with a few leading thoughts. All through His earthly career, Jesus exercised royal authority, and showed Himself to be a king. On a few occasions He was greeted as King, as for instance by Nathanael (John 1:49), and by the multitude when He rode into Jerusalem. John 12:13. But this occasion was the only time when He declared Himself plainly to be a King. When Pilate asked Him, "Art Thou a King, then," Jesus answered, "Thou sayest it because I am a King." John 18:37, R.V., margin. And then in saying, "My kingdom is not of this world," (Verse 36), He plainly declared His kingship.

Jesus was accused to Pilate as a plotter against the Roman government, and dangerous to its peace. When Pilate sought to release Him, "the Jews cried out, saying, If thou let this man go, thou art not Caesar's friend; whosoever maketh himself a king speaketh against Caesar." John 19:12. But Jesus destroyed the force of this accusation, by declaring His kingdom not to be of this world, and stating that since it was not of this world His servants would not fight.

In delivering Jesus up to Pilate, the Jewish rulers made it very apparent that they had no real accusation against Him. When Pilate said, "What accusation bring ye against this man," they answered and said unto him, "If He were not a malefactor, we would not have delivered Him up unto thee." This is the same as though a man should be brought before a court, and when the judge asks what charges there are against him, his accusers content themselves by saying, "He is a bad man." In so saying the Jews virtually confessed that they knew nothing against Him, and that Pilate must himself find out the character of Jesus by examining Him. But Pilate on examining Jesus, said, "I find no fault in Him." And Jesus expressly disclaimed any design against the power of the Roman government.

Verses 36 and 37 define the character of Christ's kingdom and of His subjects. He is a King, but His Kingdom is not of this world. In declaring to Pilate that He was King, He said, "To this end was I born, and for this cause came I into the world, that I should bear witness unto the truth." He is King of truth because He is the truth, and therefore truly a king. For since the king is the one who is above all, whosoever is the truth must be a king; because the truth is that which is highest, and which rises above all, no matter how much it is down-trodden.

> "Truth crushed to earth will rise again,
> The eternal years of God are hers."

The truth is *that which is*; that which abides forever. God is the truth. Truth cannot be destroyed. "The world passeth away, and the lust thereof, but he that doeth the will of God abideth forever." 1 John 2:17. These facts taken together with the statement of Christ, prove that this world and the truth are in opposition; and that is shown in the very fact that Christ was on trial—it was the world against the truth. But the world passes away, while truth cannot pass away. Therefore, we find that the world is always in opposition to the truth, and thus always in opposition to Christ. The world crucifies Christ today, even as He was crucified from the foundation of the world, And it is by the cross of Christ that we are crucified unto the world and the world to us. Gal. 6:14.

Christ is the Prince of Peace. Isa. 9:6. He Himself is Peace. Eph. 2:14. He came and preached peace. Verse 17. He rules by peace. Col. 3:15, 16. It is by "the peace of God which passeth all understanding" that Christ keeps His subjects. Phil. 4:7. When talking to His disciples the very night He was betrayed, He said: "These things have I spoken unto you, that in Me ye might have peace. In the world ye shall have tribulation; but be of good cheer; I have overcome the world." John 16:33. All followers of Christ, therefore, have peace, and keep the peace, no matter how much war and trouble there may be in the world. Jesus conquered the world, not by war, but by peace; and only those who absolutely refuse to fight can conquer the world. When Christ's professed followers take up carnal weapons, they may be put to flight; indeed, the very taking of weapons is their defeat. But it is absolutely impossible to conquer the man who steadfastly and consistently and for Christ's sake refuses to fight. So long as he maintains his steadfastness, he is conqueror.

Christ says that if His kingdom were of this world, His servants would fight; but He Himself had only a few hours before sharply reproved Peter for drawing the sword, and had healed the wound made by it. Wherever, therefore, anyone makes use of weapons of warfare, he shows either that he does not understand the nature of Christ's kingdom, or that he does not rank himself among Christ's followers. Whoever fights shows himself the servant of another master than Christ, and no man can serve two masters.

Christ's kingdom is not of this world. It is of an entirely different nature from the world, and the world is opposed to it, and to Christ and to His followers. Jesus said, "If the world hate you, ye know that it hated Me before it hated you. If ye were of the world, the world would love his own; but because ye are not of the world, but I have chosen you out of the world, therefore the world hateth you." John 15:18, 19. This shows plainly that the world is opposed to and hates Christ's kingdom, because it is not of this world. Therefore it follows that it is impossible for men to be subjects of worldly kingdoms and at the same time subjects of Christ's kingdom. The followers of Christ, and the subjects of His kingdom, have of right nothing more to do with the government of this world than the subjects of the Czar of Russia have to do with the government of Great Britain.

Someone, without thinking, might declare this to be anarchy; but that would be only because they do not consider the nature of Christ's kingdom. Christ Himself was condemned as an anarchist, because the princes of this world did not understand; if they had they would not have crucified the Lord of glory. 1 Cor. 2:8. Christ's followers can never be anarchists, because the law of God is in their hearts. They represented the highest type of obedience to the law. They are perfect keepers of the perfect law. Moreover, although they do not reckon themselves as subject of this world, they are indeed the very best subjects, since they make no trouble and raise no disturbance. They are keepers of the peace, so much so that instead of resisting unjust law, they will even submit to the most unjust laws without opposition. The just are condemned and killed, but do not resist. James 5:6. Therefore the best subjects that any earthly king can have are those who profess to be and are only subjects of Christ, and not of the world. Earthly governments, however, do not as a general thing know this, and so the men whose presence tends to the strength and stability of the government, are discriminated against and persecuted.

The kingdom of Jesus is not of this world, but outlasts this world. Being of the truth, it is an everlasting dominion. Christ is set at the right hand of God in heavenly places, far above all principality, and power and might and dominion. Eph. 1:20, 21. But this place was of right His even while He was here upon earth. For when talking with Nicodemus He declared himself to be "in heaven." John 3:13. The King of the universe was on trial before an earthly court and an earthly judge; and on trial as to His right to rule. He showed His right to rule there, as everywhere, by bearing witness to the truth.

But even as Jesus is set at the right hand of God in heavenly places, far above all principalities, power, might and dominion, so has God raised all those who believe in Him, and made them sit together with Christ in heavenly places. Eph. 2:1–6. He "loved us, and washed us from our sins in His own blood, and hath made us kings and priests unto God and His Father." Rev. 1:5, 6. Therefore all Christ's subjects are kings, far higher in rank than any or all kings of this earth. Power is given them over the nations, the same as to Christ Himself. See Ps. 2:8, 9; Rev. 2:26, 27. All are called to be witnesses together with Christ. God says, "Ye are My witnesses... and My Servant whom I have chosen..." Isa. 43:10. "But ye are a chosen generation, a royal priesthood, an holy nation, a peculiar people; that ye should show forth the praises of Him who hath called you out of darkness into His marvelous light." 1 Peter 2:9.

Just as Christ the King was arraigned before the bar, so are all His followers on trial in this world. The court is continually set; the case is always on, and the witnesses are always under oath. If they are faithful and true witnesses, like the Master (see Rev. 3:14), then are they kings indeed, and are never overcome, even though condemned. By the peaceful power of simple steadfastness to truth, the followers of Christ will yet be acknowledged even by the world to have power greater than that of the whole world.

Yet will they be like Christ, reckoned among the transgressors, for the sad fact is that "judgment is turned away backward, and justice standeth afar off; for truth is fallen in the street, and equity cannot enter. Yea, truth faileth; and he that departeth from evil maketh himself a prey." Isa. 59:14, 15. Nevertheless, although the truth may be scoffed at as impractical, and its adherents mocked and persecuted and even put to death, and error will seem to triumph, yet will the truth rise above everything, even as Christ, although mocked, put to death as a malefactor and counted as nothing, arose and took His seat on the throne of God. And at no time has He ever been greater than He was when His life was traded for that of a murderer. His humiliation and shame was His glory. His weakness was His strength; and the curse of the cross was the means by which He was raised to heaven to bless the universe.

—May 18, 1899

Chapter 23
A Finished Work

John 19:17–30

Jesus had been tried, found innocent, and condemned to death. He was condemned for being the Son of God, the Jews crying out, "We have a law, and by our law He ought to die, because He made Himself the Son of God;" and yet the law itself was full of statements of God's care of *them* as sons, and of declarations that He wished to be *their* Father, and have them act toward Him as sons. Jesus was condemned for being what all ought to have been and were not.

The world knew not Jesus as the Son of God. He was born of the seed of David according to the flesh, but declared to be the Son of God with power according to the Spirit of holiness, by the resurrection from the dead. See Rom. 1:3, 4. He did not become the Son of God by the resurrection from the dead, but the resurrection was the proof, the demonstration, that He was such. He was as much the Son of God during His whole life before the crucifixion as He is now, but the resurrection is the proof of it. Even so with all who are true followers of Him. "Behold, what manner of love the Father hath bestowed upon us, that we should be called the sons of God; therefore the world knoweth us not, because it knew Him not. Beloved, now are we the sons of God, and it doth not yet appear what we shall be; but we know that when He shall appear we shall be like Him, for we shall see Him as He is." 1 John 3:1, 2. This being the case, we need not be surprised if we should receive some of the same treatment from the world, that He received.

Bearing the Cross

"And He bearing His cross went forth into a place called the place of a skull, which is called in the Hebrew, Golgotha; where they crucified Him, and two others with Him, on either side one, and Jesus in the midst." He could have refused to bear the cross, if He had wished, and none could have compelled Him. He "endured the cross, despising the shame." If we are His true followers, we shall also meekly endure what is put upon us. How often, on the contrary, we not only refuse to bear anything that we can possibly avoid, but we fret and complain over burdens and trials that we cannot escape. Thereby we not only show that we are not His disciples, but that we are positively unwilling to be His followers.

Jesus could have avoided the cross, but only by denying His mission. So we can refuse the cross, but only by denying Him. There are thousands of ways in which the world will crucify us, if we are really determined to be followers of Jesus, among which sneers, a mild pity for such impractical fanatics, or surprise that we should be content to bury our talents, and flattering invitations to "better our condition" are not the least. There will be many a specious temptation to engage in something which the world would make us believe to be perfectly consistent with our profession, but which we in our hearts know to be inconsistent. We refuse the cross of Christ, and deny Him, either by giving up the truth, or by acting contrary to its purity and simplicity.

King of the Jews

"And Pilate wrote a title, and put it on the cross. And the writing was, JESUS OF NAZARETH, THE KING OF THE JEWS. This title then read many of the Jews; for the place where Jesus was crucified was nigh to the city; and it was written in Hebrew, and Geek, and Latin. Then said the chief priests of the Jews to Pilate, Write not, The King of the Jews; but that He said, I am King of the Jews. Pilate answered, What I have written, I have written." This was a severe blow to the pride of the priests, and was all the poor satisfaction that Pilate got out of the affair.

Was this the proper title to put upon the cross, or was it a libel, which Pilate was willing enough to perpetrate in order to spite the Jews? A little thought will convince anyone that it was the simple truth. Jesus was and is the King of the Jews. When Nathanael greeted Him with the words, "Rabbi, Thou art the Son of God; Thou art the King of Israel (John 1:49), Jesus accepted it without rebuke or comment. There was nothing incongruous in the double title. As Son of God, He was also King of Israel, because God the Father makes Himself known even to us in this age, as the God of Abraham, and of Isaac, and of Jacob; and it was only in their seed that all the families of the earth were to be blessed. He always declared Himself to be the Son of David; and the angel who announced His birth to Mary, said, "He shall be great, and shall be called the Son of the Highest; and the Lord God shall give unto Him the throne of His father David; and He shall reign over the house of Jacob forever; and of His kingdom there shall be no end." Luke 1:32, 33.

It follows, therefore, that all subjects of Christ's kingdom must be Jews. All true Christians are Jews. Nowhere is Christ called the King of the Gentiles. All who are Gentiles are "without Christ, being aliens from the commonwealth of Israel, and strangers from the covenants of promise, having no hope, and without God in the world." Eph. 2:11, 12. All Christians must cease to be Gentiles, and become Jews. Then is Christ indeed their King. "Salvation is of the Jews." John 4:22. Let no one therefore despise that portion of the Scriptures which was committed especially to the Jews. In it we find salvation and eternal life.

Dividing the Spoil

"Then the soldiers, when they had crucified Jesus, took His garments, and made four parts, to every soldier a part; and also His coat; now the coat was without seam, woven from the top throughout. They said therefore among themselves, Let us not rend it, but cast lots for it, whose it shall be; that the Scripture might be fulfilled, which saith, They parted My raiment among them, and for My vesture they did cast lots."

Even so must it be done with Christ's followers, when they become perfect representatives of Him. The reason why it is not done now is that, while there are true followers of Jesus, in whom His life is perfectly reproduced, they are so very few that they attract no notice. In the church as a whole the life of Jesus is not manifested. Among the great majority of professed followers of Christ, anyone who should be just as Christ was in the world, would be counted a fool and a fanatic, and thus is Jesus Himself condemned. Men think that they are followers of Christ, although they know that they do not do as He did; but they explain the incongruity, and satisfy their consciousness, by saying that times are different now from what they were then; the circumstances are so different that Christianity is obliged to adopt itself to them; but the principle is the same. This is but a delusion of the devil. The world is just the same now that it was then, and Jesus Christ is exactly the same. So when the life of Jesus is perfectly reproduced in His followers they will share His sufferings and humiliation. "The disciple is not above his Master, nor the servant above his Lord. It is enough for the disciple that he be as his Master, and the servant as his Lord. If they have called the Master of the house Beelzebub, how much more shall they call them of His household?" Matt. 10:24, 25.

Therefore, since we are living in the last days, when the Son of man may be expected to return, and therefore when the work of the Gospel must be consummated, all those who give themselves to the Lord, to serve Him, and to keep His commandments, must do so with the understanding that it is to cost them all their worldly property. There have been those who took joyfully the spoiling of their goods (Heb. 10:34), and even so must it be again. In this we can see that Christ's followers are not to amass wealth for themselves. Whoever becomes really and truly a disciple of Christ, realizing that he must become as poor in this world's goods as was the Master, will never let considerations of property stand in the way of his obeying any truth of God.

Each the Distributor of His Own

It is always much easier and pleasanter for a man to dispose of his own property than for another to do it for him. Therefore the lesson that should be learned from the division of Christ's garments is that it is best for Christians themselves to do the "spoiling" of their goods, rather than to leave it to be done by force. When they came to seize Christ's goods, they found nothing except the clothes that He had on, and these were plain. Happy will those be who are in a similar condition when the decree goes forth that no man may buy or sell save he that has the mark, or the name of the beast, or the number of his name. See Rev. 13:17. Christians should learn to do their own dividing. In like manner they should not defer their gifts of property to the cause of God until they are dead. There is no virtue in giving that which one no longer has any use for, and which one must necessarily leave. It is like giving the Lord an old, worn-out garment.

Creation Complete in the Cross

When everything had been accomplished, that the Scriptures had said should be done to Jesus, "He said, It is finished; and He bowed His head, and gave up the ghost." In those words, "It is finished," there is a world of meaning. It was not simply that His sufferings were finished; not that He was now at liberty; no, there was in it no thought of Himself. The work of God was finished in Him for the redemption of the world. The new creation was prepared for all, and nothing could deprive them of it. The cross of Christ is the power of God (1 Cor. 1:18), and that power is creative power. Rom. 1:20. The cross creates. In Christ all things are to be restored as they were in the beginning, when everything that God had made was "very good," and man—perfect man—had dominion over all. The work of God was finished from the beginning of the creation (Heb. 4:3), and therefore the rest was ready. The proof of this is seen in the fact that "God did rest the seventh day from all His works." Verse 4. Finished work necessarily brings rest. In Christ creation is renewed, so that He offers rest to all who will come to Him. Matt. 11:28. He gives the same rest that God gave man in the beginning, and the sign of it is the same. The Sabbath of the Lord is the sign and seal of the cross of Christ.

The Law Established

Christ came to do the law of God. Ps. 40:7, 8. To the Father He said, "I have finished the work which Thou gavest Me to do." John 17:4. So the words, "It is finished," indicated that in Him the law had found its perfect fulfillment. But this shows the absolute perpetuity and immutability of God's law. God is not less wise than a man, and no man spends time and strength, and suffers pain, to accomplish a work in order that he may immediately destroy it. The more labour the work costs, the longer it is expected to stand. It cost the life of the Son of God, to do the perfect works of the law; that life was of infinite value; therefore the law will endure to eternity.

Accepting the Law in Christ

Since a finished and perfect work stands, it follows that all who accept Christ must accept the law of God to be manifested in their lives. Let no one say that since Christ perfectly fulfilled the law, therefore we have no need to keep it. He finished the work in order that we might keep it. In Him the law exists in its perfection, and therefore whoever receives Him must also receive the perfect keeping of the law. "Do we then make void the law through faith? God forbid; yea, we establish the law." Rom. 3:31. The law is the perfection of the character of Christ. Whoever finds it a hardship to keep the law, thereby proclaims his dissatisfaction with Christ; and whoever reviles and rejects the law, is at the same time reviling and rejecting Christ. Why should one wish to do so? If we ourselves were required to exhibit in our lives all the virtues of the law, then we might well complain, for they are not only contrary to the desires of the natural man, but impossible of performance. Rom. 8:7. But "it is God which worketh in you, both to will and to do of His good pleasure." Phil. 2:13. By the blessed will power of Christ, we may be made both willing to do the law, and doers of it. He not only makes us able to do the will of God, but lovers of that will. Those words, "It is finished," contain for us all the blessedness and joy and power of the new creation.

The Family of Christ

We should not close this lesson without noting that which it teaches as to the relatives of Christ, and our relation to them. As He hung on the cross, He saw His mother standing by, and also His beloved disciple John, and He said to His mother, "Woman, behold thy son! Then saith He to the disciple, behold thy mother!" John immediately recognized the relationship, by taking her to his own home. This is something more than a mere item of history. It is recorded to teach us that we stand in the closest relationship to all who are related to Christ. Jesus said, "Whosoever shall do the will of My Father which is in heaven, the same is My brother, and sister, and mother." Matt. 12:50. Therefore we are to recognize all such as our own kindred, equally with those who are our kindred by ties of blood, even by the blood of Christ. This tie also binds us to all for whom Christ died; but of course those who have accepted the sacrifice of Christ are thereby made near. "As we have therefore opportunity, let us do go unto all men, especially unto those who are of the household of faith." Gal. 6:10.

—May 25, 1899

Chapter 24

Christ Risen

John 20:11–20

If Mary and the disciples had only believed what Jesus had told them, they would not have been surprised to find an empty tomb that morning, and no tears would have been shed. He had told them "how that He must go to Jerusalem, and suffer many things of the elders and chief priests and scribes, and be killed, and rise again the third day," but other plans for Him and themselves had so occupied their minds as to shut out His words. And so it is now. Many unnecessary tears are shed because the Lord's words are not believed. But so tender is the love of the Lord toward us that He has compassion upon those who weep, even though it be unnecessarily, and He sends words of comfort and help. And so two of the angels who were even then about Mary, and who are constantly watching over us, become visible to her, and inquired, "Woman, why weepest thou?" Her answer reveals an earnest desire to know where her Lord is, and so she finds at once that He was not far from her. "She turned herself back, and saw Jesus standing, and knew not that it was Jesus."

What a pity to see Jesus and not know Him! To be within the sound of His voice, and yet not to recognize Him! Jesus asks the same question of Mary, and she is still intent upon finding the body of her Lord, little thinking that an angel had rolled away the stone and that He was alive forevermore. It took but one word to reveal the truth to her, one word spoken in the familiar tone of love, and that word was her own name, "Mary." It required but one word from her to show that her heart was still true to Him who had forgiven and cleansed her, and that word was "Master." And then having made Himself known to her, He gives her a message to the disciples, and that too in words which show that He still identifies Himself with them. Although "they all forsook Him and fled," yet He speaks of them as His brethren, and His Father is their Father, and His God is their God. And we learn from the record given by Mark that it was not sufficient to mention the disciples as a company, but Peter is singled out and referred to by name. And why? Ah, because he had denied his Lord with cursing and swearing, and he would need some special assurance that the Lord thought of him still as one of the disciples.

There can be but one purpose of His ascending to His Father immediately after His resurrection. He will receive in person the assurance that His sacrifice is accepted, and that in Him, the Man Christ Jesus, the second Adam, the human family are again brought into the Father's presence. The path to glory was by way of the cross and the tomb, and the journey has been completed. During His earthly pilgrimage He had been shut away from His Father's face, not because of His own sins but on account of the sins of these same brethren, but now He has put away sin by the sacrifice of Himself, and He, as the representative of His brethren, freed from sin, ascends to the Father.

What a meeting was that! When the *prodigal* son "was yet a great way off, his father saw him, and had compassion, and ran, and fell on his neck, and kissed him," but what a welcome shall He receive who had carried at the cost of a life of suffering and a death of shame the message of love and pardon from the Father in a prodigal world! If "there is joy in the presence of the angels of God over *one* sinner that repenteth," who can measure the joy over the triumphant completion of that work through which *all* sinners may have salvation? It was for the joy set before Him that He endured the cross, despising the shame. But this joy He shares with every one who will share with Him in the travail of soul for the lost. Sufficient reason, then, had Paul the apostle to say: "But none of these things move me, neither count I my life dear unto myself, so that I might finish my course with joy, and the ministry, which I have received of the Lord Jesus, to testify the Gospel of the grace of God."

The message was delivered by Mary, but "they, when they had heard that He was alive and had been seen of her, believed not." It is a typical experience, often realized by the messenger of good tidings. We too have heard His voice, and have come to know that Jesus lives, but often those who hear our message from Him to them believe not. Oh, for a testimony of greater power, which will carry a greater conviction to many hearts!

Jesus would give the fullest opportunity to all the disciples to know that no one has taken away His body, but that He has really risen from the dead, just according to His own word. That very night, when the disciples were assembled, although the doors were shut for fear of the Jews, yet Jesus came "and stood in the midst and saith unto them, Peace be unto you." And then "He showed unto them His hands and His side." No other one bears these evidences that He is the crucified Lord. And these wounds witnessed then, as they will to all eternity, to the love that gave its all on Calvary. "Then were the disciples glad, when they saw the Lord."

The tidings of the Lord's resurrection had been brought by Mary Magdalene to the disciples "as they mourned and wept," but they did not credit her report; afterward the two disciples, to whom the Lord had made Himself known at Emmaus, "returned to Jerusalem, and found the eleven gathered together, and them that were with them, saying, The Lord is risen indeed," "neither believed they them." It is therefore perfectly clear that the disciples were not gathered together to celebrate His resurrection, but they had persistently refused to believe that He had risen, and Jesus Himself "upbraided them with their unbelief and hardness of heart, because they believed not them which had seen Him after He was risen." The Lord Himself has never placed any special honour upon the day on which He was raised. The fact of His resurrection is the foundation of every Christian's hope, and a memorial has been provided which is appropriate to the experience. "Therefore we are buried with Him by baptism into death: that like as Christ was raised from the dead by the glory of the Father, even so we should walk in newness of life." Baptism when rightly administered appropriately symbolizes the death and resurrection of the Lord and our union with Him in that experience, but we have never been instructed to place any mark of distinction upon the day on which He was raised from the dead.

Gladness again filled the hearts of the disciples when they were convinced that they were looking upon the face of their Lord. It is always so with those who have become acquainted with the Lord. "They shall see His face and His name shall be in their foreheads." "In Thy presence is fullness of joy; at Thy right hand there are pleasures forevermore." "And it shall be said in that day, Lo, this is our God; we have waited for Him, and He will save us: this is the Lord; we have waited for Him, we will be glad and rejoice in His salvation."

But it is not necessary to wait until the Lord is revealed in the clouds of heaven before we see Him and are glad. "Blessed are the pure in heart: for they shall see God." "I have set the Lord always before me: because He is at my right hand, I shall not be moved. Therefore my heart is glad, and my glory rejoiceth." This is a present experience. And this is what prepares us for that time when He shall come in power and great glory. It is those whose hearts have not been cleansed, and who have not recognized the Lord in His dealings with them, who shall be afraid: "pangs and sorrows shall take hold of them." The experience of such in that great day is described in the following scripture: "And the kings of the earth, and the great men, and the rich men, and the mighty men, and every bondman, and every freeman, hid themselves in the dens and the rocks of the mountains; and said to the mountains and the rocks, Fall on us and hide us from the face of Him that sitteth on the throne, and from the wrath of the Lamb." Not having become acquainted with, and accustomed to, "the light of the knowledge of the glory of God in the face of Jesus Christ," He is to them a consuming fire. More desirable is it to them to be covered with the mountains than that the undimmed gaze of those eyes, which are "as a flame of fire," should be directed toward them. Now is the time to heed the word, "Look unto Me, and *be ye saved*, all the ends of the earth."

"Then were the disciples glad, when they saw the Lord." Do we long for the time when He will reveal Himself in our midst, and shall we be glad in that day? We are already in the dawning of that day. "Look up and lift up your heads; for your redemption draweth nigh."

—June 1, 1899

We invite you to view the complete
selection of titles we publish at:

www.TEACHServices.com

Scan with your mobile
device to go directly
to our website.

Please write or email us your praises, reactions, or
thoughts about this or any other book we publish at:

www.TEACHServices.com • (800) 367-1844

P.O. Box 954
Ringgold, GA 30736

info@TEACHServices.com

TEACH Services, Inc., titles may be purchased in bulk for
educational, business, fund-raising, or sales promotional use.
For information, please e-mail:

BulkSales@TEACHServices.com

Finally, if you are interested in seeing
your own book in print, please contact us at

publishing@TEACHServices.com

We would be happy to review your manuscript for free.

www.ingramcontent.com/pod-product-compliance
Lightning Source LLC
Chambersburg PA
CBHW081924170426
43200CB00014B/2819